Global Perspectives Series

Partnership Theology in Creative Access Regions

Partnership Theology in Creative Access Regions

Kenneth Shreve

GLOBAL LIBRARY

© 2017 by Kenneth Shreve

Published 2017 by Langham Global Library
An imprint of Langham Creative Projects

Langham Partnership
PO Box 296, Carlisle, Cumbria CA3 9WZ, UK
www.langham.org

ISBNs:
978-1-78368-108-2 Print
978-1-78368-863-0 Mobi
978-1-78368-862-3 ePub
978-1-78368-861-6 PDF

Kenneth Shreve has asserted his right under the Copyright, Designs and Patents Act, 1988 to be identified as the Author of this work.

All rights reserved. No part of this publication may be reproduced, stored in a retrieval system or transmitted, in any form or by any means, electronic, mechanical, photocopying, recording or otherwise, without the prior written permission of the publisher or the Copyright Licensing Agency.

All Scripture quotations, unless otherwise indicated, are taken from the Holy Bible, New International Version®, NIV®. Copyright © 1984 by Biblica, Inc.™ Used by permission of Zondervan.

British Library Cataloguing in Publication Data
A catalogue record for this book is available from the British Library

ISBN: 978-1-78368-108-2

Cover & Book Design: projectluz.com

Langham Partnership actively supports theological dialogue and a scholar's right to publish but does not necessarily endorse the views and opinions set forth, and works referenced within this publication or guarantee its technical and grammatical correctness. Langham Partnership does not accept any responsibility or liability to persons or property as a consequence of the reading, use or interpretation of its published content.

CONTENTS

	Abstract	xi
	List of Charts and Tables	xiii
	Abbreviations	xv
1	**Background Study**	1
	Introduction	1
	The Researcher	2
	Statement of the Problem	3
	Purpose of the Study	4
	Research Questions	4
	Significance of the Study	4
	Delimitations	4
	Limitations	5
	Assumptions	5
	Definitions	5
	Summary	7
2	**Literature Review**	9
	Introduction	9
	Theoretical Background	9
	Thematic Background	22
	Methodological Background	46
	Summary and Research Direction	47
3	**Research Design and Methodology**	49
	Introduction	49
	Archival Method	50
	Survey Method	51
	Summary	56
4	**Partnership and the Trinity**	57
	Introduction	57
	The Trinity: An Overview	57
	The Trinity: Unity and Relationship	63
	The Trinity: Diversity in Roles	65

	The Trinity: Together in Action 72
	Summary and Reflection................................. 74
5	**Partnership and the Purpose of God...................... 75**
	Introduction 75
	God's Overall Purpose.................................. 75
	God's Purpose in the Old Testament...................... 84
	God's Purpose in the New Testament 87
	Summary and Reflection................................. 91
6	**Partnership and the Body of Christ........................ 93**
	Introduction 93
	The Body of Christ and the Trinity 93
	The Body of Christ: Metaphors 94
	The Body of Christ: Principles 97
	The Body of Christ: Interpersonal Relationships............ 103
	The Body of Christ: Working Together.................... 105
	Summary and Reflection................................. 116
7	**Partnership and the Gifts of the Spirit 119**
	Introduction 119
	The Gifts: Based in the Trinity 119
	The Gifts and Grace.................................... 121
	The Gifts: A List 122
	The Gifts: Their Purpose 125
	The Gifts: Their Scope 126
	Summary and Reflection................................. 130
8	**Partnership and the Church 133**
	Introduction 133
	The Church and the Trinity 133
	The Church: Definition of *Ekklesia* 134
	The Church: Forms of *Ekklesia*.......................... 136
	The Church: Local versus Universal Debate................ 141
	The Church in All Its Forms in the CAR 150
	The Church: A Practical Example 157
	Summary and Reflection................................. 159
9	**Survey Results and Analysis 161**
	Introduction 161
	Survey Overview 161

	Tables of Response Scores	162
	Demographic Information	167
	Open-Ended Questions	169
	Summary	171
10	**Conclusions and Recommendations**	**173**
	Introduction	173
	Conclusions	173
	Recommendations for Future Studies	176
	Appendix: CARN Survey	**179**
	Bibliography	**183**

Abstract

This study was motivated out of a desire to explore the theological issues that under-gird partnership in missions today. Strategic partnerships are becoming more and more prominent in different regions of the world. There have been tremendous spiritual gains as a result of this type of collaboration. This study seeks to address the issue of "why" believers should collaborate together.

The study is undertaken in the context of a specific Creative Access Region (CAR). Two key questions guide the study. The first asks what specific theological issues inform partnership in Christian missions in the CAR. The second asks how workers in the CAR interact with those theological issues.

The five theological issues explored as they inform partnership are the Trinity, the Purpose of God (*missio Dei*), the Body of Christ, the Gifts of the Spirit, and the Church – both local and universal. The central interpretive motif for a theology of partnership flows out of the first theological issue, the Trinity. The Trinity is seen as relationship, and this motif of Trinity/relationship permeates the dissertation.

The study used an integrated approach, combining archival and survey methods. The archival method was used for the biblical/theological material. Theology is done in community; therefore, a survey was used to have attendees of the CAR Consultation reflect on these theological issues in the context of partnership in CAR.

The results of the study revealed strong biblical/theological support for collaboration in missions in the context of the Creative Access Region.

LIST OF CHARTS AND TABLES

Chart A: The Triune God 61
Chart B: Koivisto's View of the Universal Church 151
Chart C: Individual Believers Connected Outside the CAR 152
Chart D: Local Churches in the CAR 153
Chart E: The Church in the CAR 154
Chart F: Universal Church's Impact on the CAR 155
Chart G: Partnership Examples in the CAR 156
Chart H: Distribution Comparison 162
Chart I: Representation 167
Chart J: Delegates' Home Continents 168
Chart K: Where Delegates Live 169
Chart L: First Time Attendees 170

Table 1: Information Needs Matrix 54
Table 2: Participation of the Persons in the Godhead 73
Table 3: Frequency Distribution for Questions 1–22 163
Table 4: Grand Tour 164
Table 5: Trinity 164
Table 6: Mission 165
Table 7: Body 165
Table 8: Gifts 166
Table 9: Church 166

Abbreviations

AWEMA: Arab World Evangelical Ministers Association

CAR: Creative Access Region

CARC: Creative Access Region Consultation

CARN: Creative Access Region Network

COMIBAM: Cooperación Misionera Iberoamericana

CWME: Commission and Division of World Mission and Evangelism

IMC: International Missionary Council

LOP: Lausanne Occasional Paper

MANI: The Movement for African National Initiatives

SEALINK: South East Asia Unreached Peoples Network

UCCP: United Church of Christ Philippines

USPG: United Society for the Propagation of the Gospel

WEA: World Evangelical Alliance

WEF: World Evangelical Fellowship

WCC: World Council of Churches

1

Background Study

Introduction

Within certain regions of the world, such as one that we will refer to as the Creative Access Region (CAR), there is yet to be a significant church birthed among the local population. For the last 1,400 years, a dominant non-Christian religion has ruled the region. There is no visible local church – only a handful of house fellowships and some scattered believers in the entire region. In the last several decades the demographics have greatly changed, as there has been incredible growth and expansion. Expatriates from all over the world have flocked to this region to meet the needs of the booming economies. What once was a closed and forsaken part of the world has now become center stage. Among the foreign workers streaming into this region is a huge expatriate Christian population, which is made up of believers from many nations and denominations from all over the world. A growing number of intentional tentmakers are also coming, with the purpose of sharing the gospel of Jesus with the local population. Most are working with Western missions agencies. With the present shift of political and economic ties to the Far East, more and more tentmakers are coming from countries such as Singapore, China, and the Philippines. This has raised awareness in the Far East of missions to the CAR. There is a growing interest and a fresh commitment to prayer.

There is a large expatriate church in the CAR, with as many as one million Christians from a Protestant Evangelical background living just within a few CAR nations. Since the turn of the century, there have been exciting new opportunities for the indigenous peoples to hear the gospel of Jesus Christ. Media has played the central role. For fifty years, radio was the main source of information for anyone seeking to know more about Christianity. Today, there is the Internet, with literally hundreds of web sites and chat rooms. There are several CAR-language Christian satellite programs being beamed directly into the region, which creates opportunities for CAR nationals to view programs in the privacy of their homes. Christians who have flocked to these lands from around the world are found at every level of society, as housekeepers, store clerks, and businessmen and women. Myriads of expatriate fellowships have sprung up. Some have buildings and recognition from the government. Some have trained clergy and relationships with denominations back in their home countries.

Many other small fellowships meet along language and cultural lines and have no officially trained leadership. There is an expatriate CAR-language church made up of believers from Christian backgrounds from nearby countries, which are also dominated by the same non-Christian religion. It is obvious that in these days God has raised up a Christian presence, but only a few of these expatriate churches are interested in sharing the gospel with those outside their own community. The Great Commission task of sharing the gospel still remains. There is a need for all of these converging Christian entities to have a biblical understanding of what it means to be brothers and sisters in the family of God and what part they have to play in fulfilling God's Great Commission. Many will not be able to address the question of "How can we work together?" until they are convinced of the biblical truths of "Why we should work together."

The Researcher

The topic of partnership in the Great Commission and, more specifically, in the CAR and neighboring regions, is one of the most significant topics in my life. My journey with the Lord began when I was twelve. By the time I had graduated from high school, I knew that I wanted to know him more than anything else. I enrolled in a Bible school and eventually, after several years and a few different schools, graduated with a Master's of Divinity. For the last twenty-four years, my wife and I have ministered in the CAR and neighboring regions with an agency, raising our two children overseas. In all of our time in these regions, we have been closely connected to the local church, in whatever form that happened to take.

The burning issues for me over the last fifteen years have been the unity of the body of Christ and the coordination of missions for the sake of the gospel.

This focus would include agency-to-agency, church-to-church, and church-to-agency relationships. As I worked with agencies, churches, and partnerships, the personal relationships developed within these often-separate spheres not only enabled me to understand some of the hindrances to partnership, but more importantly, to see the awesome potential of what can be done when there is unity and a desire for collaboration. This is the fire that burns within me: that God may be known in the CAR and neighboring regions and that his people would function as his body. God, in his sovereignty, has brought me on a journey where my background includes biblical-theological training and on-the-ground experience.

Statement of the Problem

Although there is a huge expatriate Christian community, many Western missions agencies, and a growing Far East contingent, there is very little cooperation among these entities on the ground in the CAR for the sake of sharing the gospel with the indigenous population. A CAR Partnership has been successfully formed, but it is a small entity among the huge expatriate Christian population. There are racial, national, theological, organizational, and ecclesiological differences that keep potential colleagues apart. This lack of cooperation has, at best, slowed the pace of the gospel going out and, at worst, actually hindered it.

Much research has been done on the practical side of partnership and the "how to" of working together. However, there is a need for theological reflection on key issues that pertain to partnership in the context of the CAR. There are expatriate churches that have no concept of their responsibility for reaching the locals. Other expatriate churches see their church as *the* church; if anything goes on in terms of ministry, it must be through them. There is a lack of acknowledgement of the Great Commission and the body of Christ as it applies to other churches. Many churches have no acknowledgement of mission agencies and their vision and passion for reaching the indigenous peoples. At the same time, there is a very weak appreciation of the huge expatriate church population on the part of the mission agencies. Added to this is a growing missions movement coming out of the Global South that is appearing on the scene with its own ideas of how to reach the CAR nationals. Media churches are being formed; new indigenous believers find their fellowship and identity with those in chat rooms and with personnel in radio and television programs. There is a need for a biblical basis of working together as the body of Christ in the specific context of the CAR. There is a need for theological reflection by the workers in the CAR in the area of partnership in Christian missions.

Purpose of the Study

The purpose of this study is to conduct an integrated research combining archival and survey methods towards the formulation of a missiological theology of partnership in Christian missions in the CAR context in order that the body of Christ may be encouraged to greater cooperation in the accomplishment of the Great Commission.

Research Questions

There are two overriding research questions guiding the process of the research.

1) What specific theological issues inform partnership in Christian missions in the CAR?
2) How do workers in the CAR interact with those theological issues?

Significance of the Study

The significance of this study will be in two areas.

1) It will add to the body of research informing a theology of partnership in Christian missions.
2) It will engage workers in the CAR in theological reflection on five key theological issues as they pertain to partnership in Christian missions in the CAR.

Delimitations

1) This study is focused on biblical principles of partnership as they apply to Christian missions in the CAR and not primarily on secular collaboration principles.
2) This study is confined primarily to evangelical sources.

3) This study will focus on theological foundations of partnership in Christian missions and not on the practical steps of implementation.

4) The survey population is limited to those in attendance at the 2009 CAR Consultation (CARC), which is held each year by the CAR Network (CARN).

Limitations

1) The researcher recognizes time restraints in the ability to complete the research and the need to be in the USA to have access to archival materials.

2) The literature researched will be in the English language only.

Assumptions

1) The Holy Scriptures are inspired and authoritative.

2) The grammatical-historical method is valid for interpretation of Scripture.

3) The study of God's Word will reveal truth and provide guiding principles that can be applied today in the area of partnership in missions.

4) The process of theology is done in community.

5) Archival research alone will not be sufficient to inform a theology of partnership in the CAR context. Therefore, the survey method will be used to compliment the archival research.

Definitions

Creative Access Region (CAR): The geographical region made up of the countries that this study was based on, where there is a non-Christian dominant religion, no recognized indigenous church, and no missionary activity allowed.

Theology: "The sustained effort to know the character, will, and acts of the triune God as he has disclosed and interpreted these for his people in Scripture, to formulate these in a systematic way in order that we might know him, learn to think our thoughts after him, live our lives in his world on his terms, and by thought and action project his truth into our own time and culture."[1]

Integrated Research Method: "A class of research where the researcher mixes or combines quantitative and qualitative research techniques, methods, approaches, concepts or language into a single study."[2]

Missio Dei: I accept Bosch's definition: "... (God's mission), that is, God's self-revelation as the One who loves the world, God's involvement in and with the world, the nature and activity of God, which embraces both the church and the world, and in which the church is privileged to participate. *Missio Dei* enunciates the good news that God is a God-for-people."[3]

Mission & The Purpose of God: In this study they are used interchangeably and defined as the *missio Dei,* God's mission in all its fullness for the salvation of mankind.

Missions: The expansion of the kingdom of God by the body of Christ through various means and methods in collaboration with the Triune God to accomplish the *missio Dei.*

Missiology: "Missiology is the science of missions. It includes the formal study of the theology of mission, the history of missions, the concomitant philosophies of mission and their strategic implementation in given cultural settings."[4]

Partnership: The unique opportunities in working with the Triune God and the body of Christ to accomplish the *missio Dei* under the power and direction of the Holy Spirit.

---

1. John D. Woodbridge and Thomas Edward McComiskey, eds., *Doing Theology in Today's World* (Grand Rapids, MI: Zondervan, 1991), 172.

2. R. Burke Johnson and Anthony J. Onwuegbuzie, "Mixed Methods Research: A Research Paradigm Whose Time Has Come," *Educational Researcher* 33, no. 7, October 2004, <http://carbon.videolectures.net/2009/uni_lj/fdv/ssmt09_ljubljana/onwuegbuzie_mmr/MixedMethods.ER.pdf> (accessed 3 October 2009), 9.

3. David J. Bosch, *Transforming Mission: Paradigm Shifts in Theology of Mission* (Maryknoll, NY: Orbis Books, 1991), 10.

4 John Mark Terry, Ebbie Smith, and Justice Anderson, *Missiology* (Nashville, TN: Broadman & Holman Publishers, 1998), 8.

Theology of Partnership in Christian Missions: The study of the presence and intention of the Triune God in the collaboration with his body for the salvation of mankind.

Summary

There is an awesome opportunity right now for the advancement of the gospel in the CAR. God, in his sovereignty, has brought thousands of Christians into this region of the world. They come with a variety of backgrounds that represents a rich diversity. There are multiple agencies and churches around the world seeking to engage in ministry in CAR. There is a huge influx of media ministries, such as satellite television and the Internet. This study seeks to work towards a missiological theology of partnership in Christian Missions in CAR by examining key theological issues that inform partnership in Christian missions and by engaging the attendees of the CARC, held in a CAR city, November 2009, to reflect on those theological concepts in the context of ministry in the CAR. The anticipated end result is that this research will enlighten God's people in the CAR on the concept of partnership and lead to greater collaboration for the sake of the gospel. The coming chapter reviews the literature that has been written on partnership for Christian missions.

2

Literature Review

Introduction

The idea of partnership in mission has been growing and developing for over a hundred years. The last thirty years have seen a massive growth in the interest and application of partnership principles, with new partnerships and networks being developed around the world. This literature review is divided into three sections. The first is the theoretical background, dealing with theology and missiology. The second section deals with the thematic background of partnership and explores the history, biblical principles, practical procedures, and potential partners of partnership in missions. The final section deals with the methodological background of how others have researched partnership. The chapter ends with a summary and statement of the research direction for this dissertation.

Theoretical Background

Back in 1936, Colin Cline wrote a small book called *A Manual of Christian Theology*. In it, he expounds on the idea that each generation needs to rethink its theology. Times change, and new problems arise, which influence theological reflection.

> Thus it becomes incumbent upon each generation to rethink its theology, not for the purpose of getting away from the old standards, but for the purpose of adjusting their work to the new

problems which arise, and uncovering those phases of truth that have not been given due place by those who have gone before.[1]

Context is very important. Those living within a specific context experience the world in their own unique way. Each Christian, no matter who he is or where he lives, is interacting with God and the Scriptures within his life context. Grenz states, "Every Christian is a theologian. Whether consciously or unconsciously, each person of faith embraces a belief system. And each believer, whether in a deliberate manner or merely implicitly, reflects on the content of these beliefs and their significance for Christian life."[2] This study has a unique context. It focuses on the present situation in the CAR. The question is how to theologize in this context. This section takes a look at that process. A brief overview of theology, missiology, methods of theology, and the Trinity/relationship motif will be presented.

Definition of Theology

Paul Hiebert states that, "Theology is the systematic and historical explication of the truths of the Bible."[3] Lewis and Demarest explain, in their book *Integrative Theology*, that:

> The root meaning of the word "theology" is the organized study (logos) of God (theos). However, in this work we do not claim to know anything about God apart from God's disclosure of himself in nature and in Scripture. As used here, therefore, theology is the topical and logical study of God's revealed nature and purposes.[4]

The point about revelation is an important one. It is only when God chooses to reveal himself that man can actually understand anything about God. This demonstrates God's desire for relationship with his creation. According to Erickson, the word "theology" simply means the study of God or the science of God. He goes on to give a more detailed definition, stating it is "that discipline which strives to give a coherent statement of the doctrines

---

1. William W. Klein, Craig L. Blomberg, and Robert L. Hubbard, *Introduction to Biblical Interpretation* (Nashville, TN: Thomas Nelson, 2004), 9.

2. Stanley J., Grenz, *Theology for the Community of God* (Nashville, TN: Broadman & Holman, 1994), 2.

3. Paul Hiebert, *Anthropological Insights for Missionaries* (Grand Rapids, MI: Baker, 1985), 197.

4. Gordon R. Lewis and Bruce A. Demarest, *Integrative Theology* (Grand Rapids, MI: Zondervan, 1996), 23.

of the Christian faith, based primarily on the Scriptures, placed in the context of culture in general, worded in a contemporary idiom, and related to issues of life."[5] Therefore, in his view, theology is biblical, systematic, cultural, contemporary, and practical.

Theology is considered a science, but I would also claim that theology is relational. It is done in conjunction with the living God. It is the Holy Spirit that inspired the writers to pen the Scriptures (2 Tim 3:16), and it is the power of the Holy Spirit that allows man to understand what was sent to him (John 14:26; 16:13). David Wells writes:

> For theology is the sustained effort to know the character, will, and acts of the triune God as he has disclosed and interpreted these for his people in Scripture, to formulate these in a systematic way in order that we might know him, learn to think our thoughts after him, live our lives in his world on his terms, and by thought and action project his truth into our own time and culture.[6]

There is a clear progression within these three definitions, each one adding a new element to enrich the discussion. Erickson added culture and application, and Wells added the relational aspect between man and the Triune God. Theology has developed over time, and the next section looks at that development.

Development of Theology

Tracing some of the history of theology reveals that, during the time of the enlightenment, theology was divided into four major subsections. These were biblical studies, systematic theology, church history, and practical theology. The study of missions landed in the category of practical theology. The logic behind this was that it represented the church that existed in "foreign parts."[7] This, for the most part, is where missions remains today: as a subset of practical theology. This was an unfortunate development, as it took the idea of missions out of the mainstream theological discussions and relegated it to a second-class status. Nussbaum picks up the story:

---

5. Millard J. Erickson, *Christian Theology*, 2nd ed. (Grand Rapids, MI: Baker, 1998), 23.
6. Woodbridge and McComiskey, *Doing Theology*, 172.
7. John Corrie, ed., *Dictionary of Mission Theology: Evangelical Foundations* (Downers Grove, IL: InterVarsity, 2007), 380.

When the modern missionary movement emerged and the study of mission was called for, it was at first treated as a subtopic of practical theology. Gradually through the efforts of missiologists like Gustav Warneck and Josef Schmidlin, missiology came to be recognized as a new theological discipline distinct from the other four listed above.[8]

Voices, like those of George Peters, David Bosch, and, more recently, Christopher Wright, have cried out that the mission of God should not be a subset of anything. Instead, they view mission as the very essence of God and his revealed word, and, therefore, it should take preeminence. George Peters writes:

> Missionary theology is not an appendix to biblical theology; it belongs at its very core. No doctrine of God, Christ or the Holy Spirit has been expounded completely according to the Bible until it has established the triune God as the outgoing God of mission, the God of saving purpose and relationship to mankind who undertakes a program for the progressive realization of his purpose.[9]

Bosch states:

> We are in need of a missiological agenda for theology rather than just a theological agenda for mission (:13); for theology, rightly understood, has no reason to exist other than critically to accompany the *missio Dei*. So mission should be "the theme of all theology." (Gensichen 1971:250)[10]

Wright would argue that a missiological theme provides theological coherence to the whole Bible, especially in the relationship between the Old and New Testaments. He calls for a missional hermeneutic in interpreting the Scriptures. "In short, a missional hermeneutic proceeds from the assumption that the whole Bible renders to us the story of God's mission through God's people in their engagement with God's world for the sake of the whole of

---

8. Stan Nussbaum, *A Reader's Guide to Transforming Mission* (Maryknoll, NY: Orbis Books, 2005), 134.

9. George W. Peters, *A Biblical Theology of Missions* (Chicago, IL: Moody Press, 1972), 27.

10. Bosch, *Transforming Mission*, 494.

God's creation."[11] I agree with these three writers and believe that they are correct in saying that the Triune God and his mission are at the center of the Bible and, therefore, at the center of theology. The next section deals with a definition of missiology.

Definition of Missiology

Justice Anderson, in his article "An Overview of Missiology," defines missiology as "the science of missions. It includes the formal study of the theology of mission, the history of missions, the concomitant philosophies of mission and their strategic implementation in given cultural settings."[12] There is a distinction between "mission" and "missions." The term "mission" is the *missio Dei*. "Missions" is the expansion of the kingdom of God by the body of Christ through various means and methods in collaboration with the Triune God to accomplish the *missio Dei*. Earlier in his article, Anderson explained the etymology of the word "missiology":

> . . . the term *missiology* includes the Latin *missio* referring to the *missio Dei*, the mission of God, and the Greek word λογος (referring to the λογος ἀνθρώπου, the nature of mankind). The word *missiology*, therefore, connotes what happens when the mission of God comes into holy collision with the nature of man. It describes the dynamic result of a fusion of God's mission with man's nature. It is what happens when redeemed mankind becomes the agent of God's mission; when God's mission becomes the task of God's elected people.[13]

Definitions and semantics surrounding theology are important. They create a foundation from which to start the process of looking at partnership in missions. God has called us to be in relationship with him, and this relational aspect is also an important part of the theological process. It is not just an academic exercise. One's attitude in the process is vital. Our love of God needs to be the driving force. This next section looks at the attitude one should have while attempting to do theology.

---

11. Christopher J. H. Wright, *The Mission Of God: Unlocking the Bible's Grand Narrative* (Downers Grove, IL: InterVarsity, 2006), 51.
12. Terry, Smith and Anderson, *Missiology*, 8.
13. Ibid., 2.

Attitude in Doing Theology

There is a relational aspect to theology. Grudem's consideration of the attitude one needs to have when engaging in such an important task is much appreciated. He reflects on the spiritual nature of the undertaking and explains that the study of systematic theology should include, among other things, much prayer, humility, rejoicing, and praise.[14] By focusing on these attitudes, people realize that they are deeply immersed in a relationship with almighty God and with his people. This relationship impacts the study. It impacts the reflection process. Words like "rejoicing" and "praise" are action words. They are done in direct relationship with the Godhead. The end result of theology is transformation and the application of all that has been discovered. A godly life and scriptural truth are needed in the process. Breshears says, "Theology without piety is sterile extraction. Piety without theology is empty emotionalism. Joined they are worship and truth (John 4:24)."[15] Grudem mentioned that there needs to be an attitude of humility. This is a reminder that man is sinful and lives in a fallen world. Paul Hiebert gives this warning, "The fact is, all theologies developed by human beings are shaped by their particular historical and cultural contexts – by the languages they use and the questions they ask. All human theologies are only partial understandings of theology as God sees it. We see through a glass darkly."[16] It is with some fear and trembling that one engages in the theologizing process. It is not to be taken lightly. As James states, "Not many of you should presume to be teachers, my brothers, because you know that we who teach will be judged more strictly" (Jas 3:1). In balance to that stern warning is the fact that God himself has given revelation that we may know him and his ways. He is pleased when we seek him out and seek to explore the deep parts of his nature and purpose. This is a spiritual journey that takes time and effort. David Wells writes:

> There are few lines quite so poignantly applicable to the theologian's craft as those of the medieval poet Geoffrey Chaucer, who wrote of "The lyf so short, the craft so long to lerne. Th' assay so hard, so sharp the conquering." It is, in fact,

---

14. Wayne Grudem, *Systematic Theology: An Introduction to Biblical Doctrine* (Leicester: IVP, 1994), 32–37.

15. Gerry Breshears, "THS 501E Outline: Prolegomena: Topic One – Laying the Foundation for Theology," Class Notes, Western Seminary, Portland, OR. May 2006.

16. P. Hiebert, *Anthropology*, 198.

surprising that the thought should ever cross our minds that the theological undertaking could be otherwise, for understanding – understanding of God, of ourselves, of the world – comes so slowly, so painfully slowly, that "lyf's" summer passes and the winter arrives long before this fruit is ripe to be picked.[17]

We have looked at the definitions of theology and missiology and examined the right attitude in approaching the process. It is time now to examine the method of theology.

Method of Theology

Several different scholars have outlined the important elements to any theological process. They seek to answer the question of how it is done. In their book, *Introduction to Biblical Interpretation*, Klein, Blomberg, and Hubbard set out five principles of valid theologizing.[18] They propose that:

1) Valid theologizing must follow the sound exegesis of the appropriate biblical texts.

2) Theology must be based on the Bible's total teaching, not on selected or isolated texts.

3) Legitimate theology respects and articulates the Bible's own emphases.

4) They must state theological points in ways that explain and illuminate their significance for the life and ministry of the church today.

5) Theology must be centered in what God has revealed in Scripture, not in what people, however enlightened, devise in their own thinking.

Lewis and Demarest build on this discussion through the development of their method, in which they list six successive stages:

1) Identify the problem for inquiry.

2) Identify alternative approaches to the problem that have been suggested in the history of Christian thought.

---

17. Woodbridge, 171.
18. Klein, Blomberg, & Hubbard, 462–464.

3) Formulate a summary of the relevant OT and NT passages, incorporating sound hermeneutics.

4) Order the relevant data into a coherent doctrine, relating it without contradiction to other biblical doctrines.

5) The Christian defends this doctrinal position in interaction with contrary positions in theology, philosophy, and new religions.

6) Sixth, these convictions are applied to specific life situations and ministries in the world today.[19]

Erickson, in dealing with this issue of a theological method, presents his ten steps to the process of developing a theology. It is worthwhile to look at these steps in a little more detail.[20]

1) Collection of the Biblical Materials: This includes gathering all of the relevant passages and using the best and most appropriate tools and methods for determining their meaning.

2) Unification of the Biblical Materials: This includes developing some unifying statements on the doctrinal theme, bringing the data into a coherent whole.

3) Analysis of the Meaning of Biblical Teachings: This addresses the question of "What is really meant by this body of material?"

4) Examination of Historical Treatments: This includes the examination of various interpretations. It is also meant to be a pause in the process to evaluate one's own interpretations.

5) Consultation of Other Cultural Perspectives: This provides a check to make sure that our own cultural perspective does not unduly influence the essence of the doctrine.

6) Identification of the Essence of the Doctrine: This includes "the need to distinguish the permanent, unvarying content of the doctrine from the cultural vehicle in which it is expressed."

7) Illumination from Extrabiblical Sources: The Bible is the main source for theology; however, there is a place for other sources in a limited way in the process.

---

19. Lewis and Demarest, *Integrative Theology*, 26.
20. Millard J. Erickson, *Christian Theology*, vol. 1 (Grand Rapids, MI: Baker, 1983), 70–84.

8) Contemporary Expression of the Doctrine: This is the process of taking the timeless truth and wrapping it in an appropriate contemporary meaning.

9) Development of a Central Interpretive Motif: This includes deciding on a particular theme, which is significant and helpful in looking at the whole. It will bring unity to the system and power to the communication of it.

10) Stratification of the Topics: This means to create an outline of the theology that reflects the range of topics and each item's importance within the whole. This helps define what the major issues are.

In presenting their method, Lewis and Demarest pointed out some differences with the method expounded by Erickson. They commented that Erickson's method lacks ". . . a distinctive method of decision making."[21] Their method appears to be more robust in the ability to compare results against competing alternatives. Their method is designed from the beginning to incorporate multiple views. Its focus is to be able to present a comprehensive conclusion and to defend that conclusion against the others. Their method would appear to be more appropriate for concepts that have been more developed, but in light of the relatively new nature of a theology of partnership in Christian mission, Erickson's method seems to be adequate as a guideline for this study. One of Erickson's ten points, which was not included by the other methods, focused on the need to develop a central interpretive motif. This is a significant addition, and the next section deals with that concept.

Central Motif in Theology

Erickson's ninth principle expressed the need for a central motif. This is a key concept for orienting the study. Grenz explains:

> A helpful theology incorporates what may be called a proper "integrative motif." Theology's integrative motif is that concept which serves as the central organizational feature of the system, that theme around which the systematic theology is structured. Such a motif is integrative, in that because of its location at the heart of the theological system it focuses the issues discussed and illumines the formulations of our responses to these issues.

---

21. Lewis and Demarest, *Integrative Theology*, 25.

We may term this integrative motif the "orienting concept," for it provides the thematic perspective in light of which all other theological concepts are understood and given their relative meaning or value.[22]

The main theme to which all the information of this study is oriented is that of the Trinity. Closely intertwined to the theme of the Trinity is community/relationship. The Holy Trinity dwells in community and relationship, and this is reflected in their roles within the Godhead and the works that they do as revealed in Scripture. This theme of community/relationship is a central tenet in the Trinity's relationship to mankind, mankind's relationship to the Godhead, and mankind's relationship to one another. God's extended relationship to man is demonstrated in his love for him through Christ, to the express purpose of his own glory. Mankind's response to God, his part of the relationship, is to love God through worshiping and praising him. This is the ultimate purpose of man. Missions is just a means to an end. John Piper explains:

> Missions is not the ultimate goal of the church. Worship is. Missions exists because worship doesn't. Worship is ultimate, not missions, because God is ultimate, not man. When this age is over, and the countless millions of the redeemed fall on their faces before the throne of God, missions will be no more. It is a temporary necessity. But worship abides for ever.[23]

This recognition of the glory of God and the responding praise of his people as their part in the relationship is reflected in Psalm 67:3–4: "May the peoples praise you, O God; may all the peoples praise you. May the nations be glad and sing for joy, for you rule the peoples justly and guide the nations of the earth. *Selah.*" Horizontal and vertical relationships are key in the discussion of the Godhead and missions. This Trinitarian/Relational motif sets the stage for any discussion on partnership in mission. Concerning community/relationship, Grenz writes:

> "Community" is important as an integrative motif for theology not only because it fits with contemporary thinking, but more

---

22 Stanley J. Grenz, *Revisioning Evangelical Theology: A Fresh Agenda for the 21st Century* (Downers Grove, IL: InterVarsity, 1993), 137.

23. John Piper, *Let the Nations Be Glad: The Supremacy of God in Missions* (Grand Rapids, MI: Baker, 1993), 11.

importantly because it is central to the message of the Bible. From the narratives of the primordial garden which open the curtain on the biblical story to the vision of white-robed multitudes inhabiting the new earth with which it concludes, the drama of the Scriptures speaks of community. Taken as a whole the Bible asserts that God's program is directed to the bringing into being of community in the highest sense – a reconciled people, living within a renewed creation, and enjoying the presence of their Redeemer.[24]

The overriding motif is the Trinity. Several theologians and missiologists, who will be referred to below, have claimed that this must be the starting point for interpreting Scripture and for the process of doing theology itself. The Holy Godhead is a community, existing in relationship. The Godhead was involved in creation and the redemption of man through Christ's death on the cross. It is involved in the present building of the church, and the Godhead will dwell with mankind in heaven in the eternal state. The Trinity is community, and its focus is on relationship. This relational element of God is extended to and through his church, to the praise of his great glory. Grenz continues in his discussion with a focus on the Trinity as a grand motif for his theology:

> In keeping with the classical confessional statements such as the Apostles' Creed, our systematic theology will follow a trinitarian structure. This approach is appropriate. As we have noted, because theology presupposes the presence of faith the theological enterprise develops from within the context of belief and the believing community. The faith presupposed by Christian theology is inherently trinitarian.[25]

Lesslie Newbigin also explains that the Trinity is the central motif for interpretation:

> The fundamental belief is embodied in the affirmation that God has revealed himself as Father, Son, and Spirit. I shall therefore begin by looking at the Christian mission in three ways – as proclaiming the kingdom of the Father, as sharing the life of the Son, and as bearing the witness of the Spirit. From this I shall go

---

24. Grenz, *Theology for the Community*, 30.
25. Ibid., 31.

on to look at contemporary issues in mission from the point of view of this Trinitarian faith.[26]

In their article, Wan and Hedinger bring out the importance of relationship in the Trinitarian motif. Traditionally, theologians have approached the Trinity from a technical definition mode; therefore, the questions surrounding the application of the truth of the Trinity in an individual's life or the corporate church life have been lacking.[27] They explain:

> Cunningham's first point is that trinitarian theology is not simply an invention of the Church Fathers. It is an accurate and necessary element of any description of the God revealed in the Bible. The trinitarian formulations are important because they force us to struggle with comprehending God's revelation of himself. Secondly, Cunningham points out that trinitarian study is also important because of the centrality it places on the concept of relationality. In defining the concept of personhood, for instance, modernity has assumed an autonomous individual while a trinitarian understanding of "person" sees the one in constant relation to the many (or the three).[42] A trinitarian understanding of personhood will include both the individual and the others with whom that person is involved. Cunningham's third point is that there are practical ramifications which grow from this relational view of the members of the Trinity. Specifically, it is important to develop an understanding of how the members of the Trinity relate to one another (Immanent Trinity) and how those three relate to creation (Economic Trinity).[28]

I have accepted a Trinitarian motif for theology and for this study on partnership in missions. Relationship is key to the Trinitarian motif. Therefore, it is helpful to briefly mention Wan's paradigm of relational realism.

---

26. Lesslie Newbigin, *The Open Secret: An Introduction to the Theology of Mission*, rev. ed. (Grand Rapids, MI: Eerdmans, 1995), 29.

27. Enoch Wan and Mark Hedinger, "Understanding 'Relationality' from a Trinitarian Perspective," *Global Missiology, Trinitarian Studies*, January 2006, <www.globalmissiology.org> (accessed 9 April 2008), 10.

28. Wan and Hedinger, "Understanding 'Relationality,'" 10–11.

The Paradigm of Relational Realism

The worldview paradigm of relational realism was presented as an alternative to the critical realism paradigm of Paul Hiebert. It reflects the shift happening in missions today to the Global South and the emerging church. It puts an emphasis on the Trinity, community, networking, and the vertical and horizontal relationships that mankind encounters. Wan states that, "Relationship is an essential nature within the Triune God (Father, Son and Holy Spirit) and among humanity (male and female). The reality of God's dealing with the created order is to be understood in terms of multi-level, multi-dimensional, and multi-stage reality of relationship."[29] Wan continues to define relational realism both ontologically and epistemologically. Ontologically he states that relational realism is defined as "the systematic understanding that 'reality' is primarily based on the 'vertical relationship' between God and the created order and secondarily 'horizontal relationship' within the created order." Epistemologically, Wan states that relational realism is to be defined as "the systematic understanding that God is the absolute Truth and the Perfect Knowledge, and only in relationship to HIM is there the possibility of human knowledge and understanding of truth and reality."[30] This naturally leads into a relational theology and relational missiology. Wan explains that "relational theologizing" is "systematically doing theology by way of relational approach (i.e. derived from the relational characteristic of the Trinity and 'relational realism paradigm') and its resultant theological understanding is 'relational theology.'"[31] He explains "relational missiology" as "the practical outworking of relational theology in carrying out the *missio dei* and fulfilling the Great Commission."[32] All of these concepts, relational realism paradigm, relational theology and relational missiology, are centered strongly in the Trinity. These concepts will be a tremendous help in understanding Scripture and informing the topic of this dissertation.

In conclusion, theologizing includes the following: It realizes that each person, to some extent, is a theologian and is integrating knowledge of God into his world. Times change; therefore, each generation needs to engage in

---

29. Enoch Wan, "The Paradigm of 'Relational Realism,'" *Occasional Bulletin* 19, no. 2 (Spring 2006), 1.

30. Wan, "Relational Realism," 1.

31. Enoch Wan, "Relational Theology and Relational Missiology," *Occasional Bulletin* 21, no. 1 (Winter 2007), 1.

32. Ibid.

theology for its context. Theologizing is done within the relationship man has with God. It is approached with an attitude of prayer, humility, community, and praise. It must be done with a solid methodology. The orientation of this methodology is the motif of the Trinitarian/Relationship theme, which will be the guide for the research on this dissertation topic.

The theoretical background concerning a missiological theology of partnership has laid the foundation of the theological process. It has laid the principles that the study will be based on. Having dealt with these issues, we move on to examine the thematic topic of "partnership" itself. The next section explores contemporary issues surrounding collaboration according to the four questions of the what, why, how, and who of partnership.

Thematic Background

This section is divided into four subsections: what, why, how, and who. The "what" of partnership looks at what has happened historically. The "why" of partnership deals with biblical-theological issues. The "how" of partnership deals with the practical workings of a partnership. Finally, the "who" of partnership focuses on the potential partners and their task.

The "What" of Partnership

The concept of partnership in Christian missions has been growing for a hundred years. This section traces the "what" of partnership in terms of what has taken place. This section gives a brief history of the major events surrounding the idea of partnership in mission. It covers some of the issues that emerged along the way, as Christians met together to talk about their role in the Great Commission.

At the beginning of the twentieth century, there was tremendous enthusiasm that poured over into the area of missions. In 1910 the World Missionary Conference was held in Edinburgh. This major event marked the first occasion that missionary societies began to work together.[33] There were 1,300 people present, but according to Neil only about thirty of these representatives were from the young churches.[34] The term "young churches"

---

33. Graham Alexander Duncan, "Partnership in Mission: A Critical Historical Evaluation of the Relationship between "Older" and "Younger" Churches" (Dissertation for Philosophiae Doctor in the Faculty of Theology, University of Pretoria, April 2007), 71.

34. Stephen Neill, *Christian Partnership* (London: SCM Press, 1952), 13.

referred to the emerging third-world churches or what is termed today as the Global South. John Mott was the chairman of this conference, and he expressed in several comments the positive mission outlook of the day. In the closing address, he stated, "the end of the conference is the beginning of the conquest."[35] More famously was his slogan "the evangelization of the world in this generation."[36]

Several more conferences took place prior to WWI, but the next significant meeting was the Lake Mohonk meeting of 1921. It was in this meeting that the IMC (International Missionary Council) was formed. Issues that were prominent in this conference were the relationship of missionaries to the indigenous workers, roles, decision-making, and donor funds in light of the emerging church.[37] The Jerusalem meeting of the IMC in 1928 was significant in that John Mott, who was the conference chair, called for the end of the distinction of sending and receiving churches.[38] There was a strong call for equality and for the younger churches to have full parity.

The world was changing rapidly, and WWI ended the optimistic spirit that had reigned in 1910. The next meeting of the IMC was at Tambaram in 1938. It was significant because the meeting was held in India, and, for the first time, there were more representatives from the younger churches than the older ones. Many of the discussion issues were the same as those in Jerusalem ten years earlier. The cry was still for equality between the younger and older churches.[39]

The Whitby IMC in 1947 was the first conference where the language of partnership became prominent. The Christian world was clearly seen as the sending nations of Europe and America and the receiving nations of Asia, Africa and Latin America. The phrase of this conference was "Partners in obedience."[40] Neil points out that this was the first fully international meeting of Christians since the end of WWII. The issue of the relationship between

---

35. Ken Gnanakan, *Kingdom Concerns: A Theology of Mission Today*, 1989, (Leicester: IVP, 1993), 15.
36. Gnanakan, Kingdom Concerns, 16.
37. Duncan, "Partnership in Mission," 74.
38. Bosch, *Transforming Mission*, 465.
39. Duncan, "Partnership in Mission," 76.
40. Colin Marsh, "Partnership in Mission: To Send or to Share," *International Review of Mission* 92, no. 366 (2003) (EBSCO Publishing, 2003, on Western online database, September 21, 2007), 370.

the old and young churches remained a key tension and focus of the meeting. Neil wrote:

> The Conference set out what it understood to be the prerogative of the younger Churches – "absolute spiritual equality, and of their right to manage their own affairs, to frame their own policies, and, under the guidance of God the Holy Spirit, to bear their own distinctive witness to the world, as the instrument by which God wills to bring to Christ the whole population of the lands in which they dwell."[41]

On 23 August 1948, delegates of 147 churches assembled in Amsterdam to merge the *Faith and Order Movement* and *Life and Work Movement* into what is now the World Council of Churches (WCC). This was a new movement that was parallel to, but separate from, the IMC.

The IMC meeting in Willingen, Germany in 1952 saw some major evolution. The phrase "partners in obedience" became replaced with "partnership in mission." This was the result of a renewed focus on the Trinity and seeing the mission of the Trinity, the *missio Dei*, as the main task facing the church. Colin Marsh quotes from the conference:

> The missionary movement of which we are part has its source in the Triune God himself. Out of the depths of His love for us, the Father has sent forth His own Son to reconcile all things to Himself, that we and all men might, through the Spirit, be made one in Him with the Father in that perfect love which is the very nature of God . . . There is no participation in Christ without participation in His mission to the world. That by which the Church receives its existence is that by which it is also given its world-mission. "As the Father hath sent me, even so I send you."[42]

In the mid 1950s the concept of linking Christian ministries in partnership for the sake of the gospel was not a new subject. Max Warren wrote his famous book *Partnership: The Study of an Idea*. In that book he put forth his famous statement that "Partnership is as an idea whose time has not yet fully come."[43] Colin Marsh continues on the attitude at the time:

---

41. Neil, *Christian Partnership*, 14.
42. Marsh, "Partnership in Mission," 371.
43. Max Warren, *Partnership: The Study of an Idea* (London: SCM Press LTD, 1956), 11.

More recently, Huibert van Beek acknowledged that, "Partnership is a goal, not an acquisition . . . at best it is something to be constructed, patiently, step by step," whilst Andrew Kirk has described partnership as an "idea to be aimed at." Partnership, as an ideal, has thus been distinguished from the reality of its application in mission relationships.[44]

New Delhi was the site of the third assembly of the WCC in 1961, and it was here that the IMC was formally integrated into the WCC. The IMC was given the new title of the Commission and Division of World Mission and Evangelism (CWME). The reasoning at the time was that mission and unity were paramount. The main ecclesiastical body at the time, the WCC, could not be separated from the mission task of the church. Some hoped that this would place the task of mission right at the center of the ecumenical movement.[45] There were others who saw that this would be the beginning of the end of missions, as it became swallowed up by the WCC.

The fourth meeting of the WCC was held in Uppsala in 1968. The tone of the meetings was heavily dominated by social concerns rather than the agenda of evangelism. "So instead of the CWME infusing the WCC with vision and passion for the unfinished missionary and evangelistic task, other divisions were slowly but steadily shaping the CWME to their concept of mission."[46]

In Bangkok in 1972, the issue of mission and unity was confirmed by the conference, but there was an outpouring of anger from poorer churches, and the reality was that even though "equality" was what was written in their statements, it did not reflect the reality in relationships. "Partnership in mission remains an empty slogan. Even where autonomy and equal partnership have been achieved in a formal sense, the actual dynamics are such as to perpetuate relationships of domination and dependence."[47] The issue of the dynamics of power was prominent.

In frustration at the lack of progress in the relationship between older and younger churches and the resulting friction on the ground in many mission fields, there was a call for a moratorium on missionaries from the West.

---

44. Marsh, "Partnership in Mission," 372.
45. Gnanakan, *Kingdom Concerns*, 28.
46. Ibid., 29.
47. Marsh, "Partnership in Mission," 372.

> In 1971, Rev John Gatu, General Secretary of the Presbyterian Church of East Africa, proposed the model of moratorium as one approach to redressing then imbalance which would necessitate a period of reflection on mission with the aim of transforming the unidirectional flow of resources to a multidirectional exchange where control and power would be internationalized.[48]

Although no formal moratorium came into being, this issue highlighted the tensions that still remained.

In 1974 Billy Graham had called together a new conference to be held in Lausanne, Switzerland. There were 2,700 people from over 150 countries present. In Ralph Winter's plenary address, the concept of unreached people groups was presented. Rather than this being a time in history where there would be a moratorium on workers from the West, this was a time when the whole church needed to focus on those who had never had a chance to hear the gospel. During this conference, John Stott chaired the committee that formed the influential Lausanne Covenant.

From the mid-seventies until the present, the emphasis on partnership in mission has grown. Significant movements gained momentum, such as the World Evangelical Alliance (WEA) Missions Commission. The WEA, formerly the World Evangelical Fellowship (WEF), began in the late 1800s and picked up momentum with the formation of the WCC. The WEF was the evangelical answer to the WCC. There has been a close relationship with the Lausanne movement and the WEA, with many members overlapping. Reigniting the missionary passion, the AD2000 and Beyond Movement came out of Lausanne and the WEA. It was launched from the Global Consultation on World Evangelism held in Singapore in 1989. The AD2000 and Beyond Movement believed heavily in the concept of partnership. Luis Bush, in explaining the movement, said:

> This involved the building of a new kind of partnering relationship, a "grassroots networking structure," a "grassroots movement, a network of networks, a fusion of visions" in which "we are all controlled from the bottom up rather than from the top down" with a "... focus on catalyzing, mobilizing, multiplying resources, through networks." The stated purpose was to "encourage cooperation among existing churches, movements,

---

48. Duncan, "Partnership in Mission," 86.

and entities to work together toward the vision of a church for every people and the gospel for every person by the year 2000."[49]

Although this survey was brief, it pointed out that people have been thinking about the issue of partnership for a long time. There have been massive efforts to link the worldwide church to the evangelistic task. Along the way, issues of equality, power, decision-making, influence, social agendas, and colonialism have been debated. Although Warren stated in 1955 that partnership was an idea whose time had not yet come, it can be said today in 2010 that the idea has arrived, and the tide has turned.

This section has explored the "what" – what has happened in the last hundred years in the area of partnership in missions. Today, partnership thinking stands on the shoulders of what has gone before, in terms of issues discussed and the practical results of the major conferences. The next section goes to the heart of the issue. It looks at the "why" of partnership. It deals with the biblical/theological issues that compel partnership.

The "Why" of Partnership

Prominent in the secular literature for the "why" of partnership was the concept that more could be accomplished working together than could be accomplished alone. This concept is very prominent in the Christian literature, as well. John Maxwell[50] and Panya Baba[51] referred to Ecclesiastes 4:9–12:

> Two are better than one, because they have a good return for their work: If one falls down, his friend can help him up. But pity the man who falls and has no one to help him up! Also, if two lie down together, they will keep warm. But how can one keep warm alone? Though one may be overpowered, two can defend themselves. A cord of three strands is not quickly broken.

This is a well-accepted concept. However, too often in Christian partnership meetings this "results" reason for doing partnership is the main principle put

---

49. Luis Bush, "A Brief Historical Overview of the AD2000 & Beyond Movement and Joshua Project 2000," Paper, North East Asia AD2000/Joshua Project 2000 Consultation in Seoul, 27–30 May 1996, <http://www.ad2000.org/histover.htm> (25 June 2010).

50. John Maxwell and Tim Elmore, *The Power of Partnership in the Church* (Nashville, TN: J. Countryman, Thomas Nelson, 1999), 5.

51. Panya Baba, "Chapter 11: A Two-Thirds World Perspective: A Case Study," in *Partners in the Gospel: The Strategic Role of Partnership in World Evangelization* (Wheaton, IL: Billy Graham Center, c. 1992), 109.

forth. Although true and important, it is not the main thing. This section looks at the theological "why" of partnership.

It starts with the Trinity. McKaughan,[52] Warren,[53] Hahn,[54] and Taylor[55] and many others highlighted the doctrine of the Trinity. The Godhead (its relationship, love, and unity–diversity) was seen as the starting point for understanding partnership. Although I had been involved in partnership for over a decade and heard about the Trinity in connection with partnership, it was not until interacting with the reading that this truth began to sink into my life. The more I read and prayed, the more I understood that the Trinity was not just the key to partnership but to life itself. This motif is not just the starting point for understanding partnership, but it is the overriding motif in understanding partnership and God's purpose in the world today, as stated in the previous section dealing with theology.

A. B. Simpson wrote over a hundred years ago on partnership. I believe he caught the essence and simplicity of the concept. Partnership is a vertical relationship with God and a horizontal relationship with man. It is carried out within the context of the *missio Dei*. In his book *Serving the King*, Simpson states, "All our service, therefore, is simply partnership with Christ. It is Christ working his work in us."[56] Later on he states: "Our work for God is a great partnership. We are God's fellow workers."[57] In powerful simplicity, he lays out God's part in the partnership and then man's. God pays man's debt, supplies him with all the resources, entrusts to him the Great Commission, prepares each worker, prepares their work, and rewards each one in the end. On man's part, he is to recognize that the work is Gods, to recognize the necessity to do the work together, to make sure the work is done his way, and to do it in his strength. Simpson's simple description of partnership with God, at its core, recognizes, if not demands, cooperation among God's people, as believers are God's fellow workers.

---

52. Paul McKaughan, "Chapter 6: A North American Response to Patrick Sookhdeo," in *Kingdom Partnerships for Synergy in Missions* (Pasadena, CA: William Carey Library, 1994), 69.

53. Warren, *Partnership*, 38–39.

54. Geoffrey W. Hahn, "Cross-Cultural Partnerships Characterized by Grace" (Unpublished DMin Dissertation for Denver Seminary, April 2007), 24.

55. William D. Taylor, ed. "Partners Into the Next Millennium," *Kingdom Partnerships for Synergy in Missions* (Pasadena, CA: William Carey Library, 1994), 237.

56. A. B. Simpson, *Serving the King: Doing Ministry in Partnership with God* (Camp Hill, PA: Christian Publications, 1995), 13.

57. Ibid., 79.

The essence of the vertical/horizontal relationship was expounded half a century later in one of the first books on partnership written by Max Warren. In the mid-1950s, he penned *Partnership: The Study of an Idea*. This book was first published in 1956 and seems to have been ahead of its time, at least in terms of the strategic partnership movement that emerged in the 1980s.

In terms of biblical principles, Warren starts with the threefold understanding that partnership relates to the very nature of God. It relates to God's relationship with man, and it relates to man's relationship with man. He begins by pointing to the Trinity as an example of diversity and unity. It is through the love and action of the Godhead that we see his purposes being worked out. The author points to how God shares his work with man as fellow laborers (1 Cor 3:9), ambassadors (2 Cor 5:19), and his mouthpieces (Amos 3:7). Terms that are important are *koinonia* and "in Christ." Both are found throughout the New Testament, and Warren, although mentioning their importance, gives only a brief paragraph to each. Paul's partnership with others in the gospel is highlighted in Galatians 2:9 and Philippians 1:5. Warren highlighted the importance of "relationship," and this is a topic that needs to be pursued and developed throughout the study. Warren's focus on the Trinity and on believers as being co-workers was picked up and developed further through the works of Phill Butler, who has been one of the main proponents and teachers on partnership for the last thirty years.

Phill Butler gives his biblical rationale for partnerships in five points.[58] First, God's character is the source of community and cooperation; in the first eleven chapters of Genesis, God constantly refers to himself in the plural. Second, he points to the body of Christ (as found in Romans 12, 1 Corinthians 12, and Ephesians 4); it is the individual parts of the body working together for Christ's glory. Third, Scripture reveals two kinds of witness – individual and community. It is in community that God works in the world, as shown in the relationship with the nation of Israel. Fourth, the Holy Spirit of God is only released as God's people dwell in unity; he points to Psalm 133. Fifth, the credibility of the gospel is linked to how believers work together. Butler's idea of community is a central theme. This issue of community runs parallel to Warren's and Simpson's focus on both vertical and horizontal relationships. It is an issue that needs to be developed and explained in more depth. In Butler's outline, he points out the importance of the body of Christ. This will

---

58. Phill Butler, "Integrated Partnerships," in *Partners in the Gospel: The Strategic Role of Partnership in World Evangelization* (Wheaton, IL: Billy Graham Center, c. 1992), 34–35.

become a major chapter within the dissertation. As one looks at the topics Butler mentions, it becomes clear that a connecting thread is needed that ties everything together. Rather than looking at topic after topic to give a list of proofs for partnership, a motif of the Trinity and relationship/community is needed to anchor each point presented.

Bill O'Brian came to some of the same conclusions as the men above as he wrote "Cooperation in Evangelism."[59] He begins his paper with an overview of biblical support for partnership: the example of Trinity, God's working with man as revealed in the OT covenants, and the NT focus on "fellow workers." He uses the illustration of the four men carrying the paralytic man to Jesus. He assigns four attitudes to the men, each of which could destroy the mission, but they put this aside for the sake of the task. O'Brien goes on to list obstacles to working together that come from superior attitudes of individuals in the body of Christ. They are: racial and national superiority, ecclesial superiority, gender superiority, and economic superiority.

One of the most theologically astute writers today on partnership is Charles Van Engen. In his article "Opportunities and Limitations,"[60] he addresses the issue of partnership by suggesting four reasons why we need to partner together for world evangelization, gleaned from Ephesians 4:1–5:2. In summary, he states, "We work together as we follow (and co-labor with) Jesus Christ in mission in God's world in the power of the Holy Spirit."[61] The first reason is: "*Together* we belong to Jesus Christ ('together')." He points out that Paul in Ephesians uses the singular for church, and it is the Universal "capital C" Church. We belong to one body with one head. We work together because we have the same Lord and Master. The second reason is: "*Together* we belong to each other as members of the global body of Jesus Christ ('working')." There is a special set of attitudes toward one another as the body. These attitudes are reflected in Ephesians 4:1–5:2. "Paul's challenge in Ephesians 4 calls us to consider in 'humility, gentleness, and patience,' that each of us as churches and organizations belong to each other as part of the universal, global, people of God."[62] The third reason is: "*Together* we exercise our spirit-

---

59. Bill O'Brian, "Cooperation in Evangelism," *Cooperation in Evangelism I*, 1989, <http://www.lausanne.org/documents/lau2docs/204.pdf> (2 October 2007).

60. Gary Corwin and Kenneth B. Mulholland, *Working Together with God to Shape the New Millennium: Opportunities & Limitations* (Pasadena, CA: William Carey Library, 2000), 82.

61. Ibid., 85.

62. Ibid., 95.

given gifts in ministry as we participate in Christ's mission ('diversity')." In light of the global emphasis of the rest of the chapter, Van Engen uses a global hermeneutic for the gifts of the Holy Spirit. They apply to the church universal. Finally, the fourth reason: "We grow *together*, as *together* we grow into the fullness of the stature of Jesus Christ ('theological')."[63]

Much of this article came from a prior article Van Engen had written titled "Toward a Theology of Mission Partnerships." In this article he traces the history of the meaning of partnership in the twentieth century. He states the main focus of his paper:

> In this paper, I would like to suggest four biblical aspects of missionary partnering in world evangelization. Why work together? So that the world may believe that Jesus is the Christ (John 17:21). Together we can evangelize the world in our generation, using the language of the "watchword" of the Student Volunteer Movement (SVM) and Edinburgh 1910.[64]

He then continues to set out the four points taken from Ephesians, mentioned above. In the discussion on the use of spiritual gifts, paternalism is a huge issue, and he goes into some detail outlining different forms that paternalism can take. He summarizes his article by saying:

> Our partnership in mission in this new millennium must be centered in Jesus Christ, focused in the local congregation, shaped by a kingdom of God missiology, directed to a world in desperate need of Christ. We must recognize that the gospel is for everyone, be committed to cooperating together in mutuality and humility, celebrate the gifts given to each member of the global community of the King, and grow together to become mature partners, attaining together to the whole measure of the fullness of Jesus Christ our Lord.[65]

I greatly admire the work that Van Engen has done on a theology of partnership. He has explored it deeper than most and made excellent points, and his thinking on the spiritual gifts has impacted me. I would prefer, however, that partnership be centered in the Trinity rather than in Jesus Christ. I would

---

63. Ibid., 85.

64. Charles Edward Van Engen, "Toward a Theology of Mission Partnerships," *Missiology and International Review* 29, no. 1 (2001): <http://search.ebscohost.com/> (12 June 2010), 16.

65. Ibid., 33.

disagree that partnership must be focused in the local congregation. I believe that concept could actually hinder partnership. Partnership must be focused wherever and with whomever the Holy Spirit determines; that may or may not be the local congregation.

Another foundational book on Partnership is *Partnering in Ministry: The Direction of World Evangelism* by Luis Bush and Lori Lutz. This book was one of the first dealing with strategic partnerships and is a classic. It gives the big picture of what can be done through strategic partnerships as it applies to the Great Commission. Being one of the first books written on the topic back in 1990, it was a catalyst for collaboration and impacted the AD2000 and Beyond Movement. Bush and Lutz added to the partnership discussion by giving great examples of partnership, focusing on Paul and his teams and specific examples from the book of Philippians. They talk about relationships between local churches, denominations and international partnerships. There are some helpful "how to" tools of partnership included. It focuses a lot on the issue of finances in missions, including how to relate with donors and to raise money in the context of partnership. Chapter 2 deals with the biblical roots of partnership. Their first sentence focuses on the Trinity, as stated in the creation of man in Genesis, "Let us make man in our image." It reveals the Godhead working together as the model for Christians. A unique item in their book is case studies of partnerships in the New Testament. The first is the partnership formed to send out the first missionary crew of Saul, Barnabas and John Mark. The second is the special partnership between Paul and the church at Philippi. The authors go into some detail, bringing out partnership examples from the book of Philippians, which include: Partnering in the Gospel (Phil 1:3–5), Partnering in the Spirit (Phil 2:1), Unity in Partnership (Phil 2:2); Partners Help Each Other to Grow (Phil 2:4–8; 3:20; 4:21); Partnership in Suffering (Phil 3:10); and Financial Partnership (Phil 4:16). The strength of their contribution was the combination of the theological with the practical, all of it in the context of reaching the world for Christ.

John Maxwell and Tim Elmore wrote *The Power of Partnership in the Church*. This powerful and thoughtful little booklet takes quick snapshots of partnership principles from both biblical texts and everyday life. Many examples were given from the business world on how working together results in greater success. A highlight is the idea that God has invited his children to partner with him. This is seen in the passages on prayer. As Christians pray, they are partnering with God and others on the earth (Matt 18:18). The invitation is also clearly demonstrated in the Great Commission: God desires believers to join him in the task of spreading the good news. From Scriptures, examples of partnership were Nehemiah rebuilding the wall and Aaron and Hur holding up Moses' arms in prayer while Joshua fought the battle in the valley below. Maxwell gives the examples of marriage and God's working relationship with the Patriarchs. The whole idea of partnership is God's idea. A central passsage is Ecclesiastes 4:9–11. It states clearly that two are better than one and then continues beyond that concept to say that a cord of three strands is not easily broken. Core to the whole reality of partnership is love. The command is given by Jesus in John 15:12–15 to "love one another as I have loved you." Maxwell says, "Love is the highest law in partnership."[66] Within all the small snapshots given by Maxwell, one stands out above the others for me, and that is the concept of partnership in prayer. This has not been a topic that others have expounded on, and I believe it is a significant issue and should be explored further in this study.

Another prominent missions leader in the area of partnership is William Taylor. He served for many years as the chairman of the Missions Commission of the World Evangelical Fellowship (WEF). In 1994 Taylor edited *Kingdom Partnerships for Synergy in Missions*. Under the leadership of the WEF Missions Commission, a consultation was held in June of 1992 in Manila. Present were ninety-five mission leaders from thirty-five different countries. This book is a conglomeration of the papers given at the Manila consultation. In his introduction, Dr Taylor outlines the four areas of concern dealt with during the week. Part 1 addresses partnership foundations and structures. Part 2 explores critical issues in partnerships, such as culture, control in church/mission relationships, and, finally, accountability in Christian partnerships. Part 3 examines internationalizing agencies. Part 4 gives seven case studies of partnership models. Biblical principles that were touched on in the different papers include: power in unity (Ps 133), the concept of the body of Christ (Rom 12, 1 Cor 12, Eph 4), synergy and leveraging of resources (Matt 25:14–30), the concept that God dwells in unity and relationship and that man was made for dwelling in relationship, believers are agents of reconciliation (2 Cor 5), witness is done by individuals and community (John 17), partnership is family (Eph 2:19), and diversity is part of partnership (1 Cor 12:14–26). In his conclusion, Dr Taylor sums up partnership by saying that it is God's idea; it originates from him as displayed in the Trinity. As God works to fulfill his purposes on earth, he chooses to partner with man to get it done.

---

66. Maxwell and Elmore, *Power of Partnership*, 95.

Paul Sampley wrote *Pauline Partnership in Christ*. The purpose of Sampley's study is to focus on the "identification and analysis of Paul's use of the *societas* partnership as a model of Christian community."[67] He argues that the concept of *societas* was a commonplace of Roman law. He explores the influence of this existing concept on Paul's use as applied to Christians and used in phrases such as "in Christ." Sampley concludes that the Jerusalem council reflects this consensual partnership (Gal 2:1–10), where James, John, Barnabas, and Cephas form a partnership for the spread of the gospel. In the book of Philippians, he points out the partnership established by Paul with the church for the sake of the gospel and how this particular partnership went so far as to include sharing of resources. In the book of Philemon, Paul urges Philemon to remain in partnership with him and to accept back the run-away slave, Onesimus. Finally, Sampley points out that the language of the *societas* is reflected in such terms as *koinonia* and phrases, such as "be of the same mind" and "agree with one another." The concept of partnership or *societas* is reflected in the mission of spreading the gospel to the whole world and also in the responsibility of believers one to another.

In the past decade, there have been dissertations written on specific aspects of partnership, either within a specific geographical region or related to a particular biblical truth. Geoffrey Hahn wrote a dissertation on "Cross-Cultural Partnerships Characterized by Grace." The core of the research was a six-session workshop that was provided for twenty-two SIM missionaries, plus two other missionaries connected with the SIM team from Ecuador. The participants were asked to think about who they could partner with to help attain their goals in Ecuador. These ideas, along with the pre- and post-workshop surveys, and the twice-monthly follow-up conversations during a three-month period, constituted the qualitative and quantitative data that was to be studied. The author begins with the Trinity. The Godhead functioning together is the foundation and model for his people. Fellowship, or *koinonia* in Greek, is a main biblical principle used to describe community and the act of working together. Several brief examples of partnership, such as the first missionary team from Acts, are considered. He then goes on to develop a Pauline theology of partnership by analyzing three passages: Ephesians 1:4–10, Corinthians 12, and Ephesians 4:1–6. Grace is a key theme of Ephesians.

---

67. J. Paul Sampley, *Pauline Partnership in Christ* (Philadelphia, PA: Fortress Press, 1980), x.

God set forth his purpose to unite everything in Christ, and it was grace that accomplished it.

This focus on grace reveals how believers should relate to one another and the truth of the worldwide unity of God's people. 1 Corinthians 12 deals with the issue of unity and diversity, which is fundamental to Christian community. Central to this passage are verses 4–6, which link different kinds of gifts, service, and work with the three persons of the Trinity – Spirit, Lord, and God, respectively. In Ephesians 4:1–6, Paul gives the exhortation to walk in unity. It is a reflection of the grace and reconciliation that has been poured out in their lives and is linked with the Trinity as one Spirit, one Lord, and one God and Father of all. The conclusion of the study is that the focus on partnership through the workshop did, indeed, increase the understanding of the importance of partnering. Central to the study is the concept of grace, which enabled people to persevere in partnership. Theological themes explored during the workshop were grace, community, power, trust, and use of gifts. Because of the focus on only three passages, the author suggests in his conclusion that much more needs to be done in the area of developing a theology of partnership. Future research suggestions included a theology of all Paul's writings, the NT or the entire Bible.

In conclusion, the "why" of partnership was explored. There was deep conviction from the authors that partnership is rooted in the very nature and character of God. Almost every author referred to the Trinity. The relationship, unity and diversity demonstrated there gave a starting point for Simpson, Warren, Butler, and Taylor. There was a strong emphasis on both vertical and horizontal relationships. The body of Christ was highlighted by Taylor and Butler as a key reason for partnership. Van Engen focused on community, expressing it in the word "togetherness" as revealed in Ephesians; he also emphasized the distribution and use of spiritual gifts. Partnership, using William Taylor's words, is God's idea. We do partnership because it is his idea, born out of the character of the Godhead. As a result of the research, five important theological issues became prominent and will be the focus of this study in the context of partnership in mission. They are the Trinity, the Purpose of God, the Body of Christ, the Gifts, and the Community (Church) of God's People.

The "why" of partnership reveals the character and heart of God. He has called his people to be fellow workers with him for his glory. He has specifically revealed this through his Holy Word. Once that is understood, the next step for believers is to obey and do it. However, as with most biblical principles, this is the hard part. How do you collaborate in a multi-cultural, multi-denominational, multi-everything worldwide Christian community? The next section focuses on the "how" of partnership.

The "How" of Partnership

Much of the literature on partnership dealt with the "how to" of working together. These were practical reflections on overcoming obstacles to partnership. Specific research was done on the hindrances to partnership. Foundational practices for solid partnerships have been discovered. A core concept to partnership is the importance of building relationships and developing trust, especially in diverse cultures. There is a huge amount of literature on collaboration and how to work together in the secular world (e.g. Spekman – 2000; Mattessich – 2001; Wenger – 2002; Straus – 2002; Harvard Business School – 2002; Dent – 2004; Wallace – 2004; Brafman – 2006.) Amongst Christian writers, there are several books (e.g. Williams – 1979; Kraakevik – 1992; Elmer – 1993; Taylor – 1994; Addicott – 2005; Rickett – 2000; Bush – 2002; Butler – 2005; Livermore – 2009; and Lederleitner – 2010.) Other important figures have written multiple articles on partnership, including Alex Araujo, Mark Avery, William Sunderland, and David Hackett. There are several Christian websites specifically devoted to partnership, such as Vision Synergy, Power of Connecting, and Catalyst Services. The desire of this literature review is to take a look at a few of the samples from this vast amount of literature. There is much to learn from the secular world on partnership; however, this review will be limited to those that are coming from a Christian perspective and have the focus of missions in mind.

Daniel Rickett serves with Partners International and has much experience with developing partnerships. His book *Making Your Partnership Work* focuses on the practical aspects of developing joint ministries. Having one vision and purpose is central to collaboration. This is what brings people together. Having results is an important part of the collaborative venture; there is a reason for the partnership to exist. One area that the author highlights, which was helpful, was the intercultural issue. People need to learn how to collaborate across cultures. It takes effort, and, in international ministry settings, culture becomes a major factor, if not THE major factor. Collaboration is based on relationships. Relationships are core to whatever takes place.

Several groups have been prominent in the last thirty years in partnership development. Interdev, with Phill Butler and his colleagues, has been at the lead. They have focused on the practical outworking of partnerships and have been involved in the development of many strategic partnerships around the world, including CAR Partnership. Two key books are Ernie Addicott's *Body Matters* and Phill Butler's *Well Connected*. These covered specific methods of how to organize and run meetings, how to set goals, how to determine a purpose statement, how to come to a joint vision, what type of structure is best, how to deal with conflict management, and dealing with diverse cultures, accountability systems, control, and finances. All of these issues impact partnership as people from different backgrounds and cultures attempt to work together. Partnership is a process and is hard work. Butler also pointed out that there are several different types of structures that can be used for collaboration purposes. There can be networks, consensus-based partnerships, and strategic alliances.[68] Some partnerships can be formed for a specific time frame (such as for a Billy Graham crusade) and others for a longer period (such as for developing Farsi radio broadcasts.) Some partnerships can be linear, such as a partnership solely dealing with delivering funds to a project; this would flow from investor to implementer to target group. Others, like integrated strategic partnerships, would be complex. An example of this would be reaching an unreached people-group with Scriptures, where several parts would be key: the people who do the translation, those who raise money for the printing, those who print the Bible, and, finally, those who distribute the new Bibles. These types tend to be messy, with more diversity and more interconnectedness.

Colin Marsh wrote an influential article titled "Partnership in Mission: To Send or To Share." This article examines the influence of partnership in mission on the United Society for the Propagation of the Gospel (USPG) between 1965 and 1996. It sought to find what influence partnership had on their mission programs and their administration. It focuses on the issue of the Western church and the one-directional sending of resources from Europe to the rest of the world. It asks the question: "Can paternalism be overcome?" Rather than the church moving from West to East, it is all churches partnering together with God in his agenda to reach the world, with everyone coming as equal partners. From this, Marsh looks at the concept of partnership and power, reflecting on the inequalities of finances and the

---

68. Phill Butler, *Well Connected* (Waynesboro, GA: Authentic Media, 2005), 42–43.

differences in culture. He raises the question, "To send or share?" In his research of the USPG, he found that the send motif was in place. However, it was a one-way scenario; there was no reciprocation. Marsh concludes that as the USPG embraced *missio Dei* and accepted that others were equal partners in the great mission endeavor, the missions thinking and structures changed from a sending mentality to a sharing mentality. This new thinking found its way into the missions strategies and administrative structures. Marsh's article helps to highlight several hindrances to partnership. It is a good case study in that it showed that, as the biblical principles are internalized and acted upon, true partnership can take place. Practical applications to the biblical principles are needed.

When it came to case studies on implementing partnerships, there were many examples from around the world. Each one would highlight some of the specific challenges. I appreciated Jonathon Rowe's article "Dancing With Elephants." His title comes from a quip made at the Iguassu dialogue, where Christians from the South describe partnership with churches and agencies from the North as akin to dancing with elephants: too big, too powerful, and too clumsy.[69] The focus of the article is on accountability. How is that done when the North has traditionally held most of the resources? He concludes that there is risk in working out accountability across cultures. The way forward is to ferment mutual trust amongst the partners. Rowe's article is helpful in highlighting key issues. However, building trust can only be accomplished as cultural understanding takes place. Various cultures will see trust and accountability in unique ways. One "how to" of partnership is to develop an environment where these cross-cultural issues can be openly and honestly discussed with the end result of mutual agreement.

Financial issues have been at the center of the issue on accountability. Mary Lederleitner addressed this issue head-on in her book, *Cross-Cultural Partnerships: Navigating the Complexities of Money and Mission.* She gives case studies to point out past mistakes and gives solid principles for moving ahead in the future. Concerning cross-cultural partnerships, she states:

> Success is not legitimate if it is at the expense, harm or detriment to any member of that body. That is our first identity, and it needs to be our first priority. It is not about meeting our own objectives, organizational ends or outcomes. It is deeper than that. It is

---

69. Jonathon Y. Rowe, "Dancing with Elephants: Accountability in Cross-Cultural Christian Partnerships," *Missiology: An International Review,* 37, no 2 (April 2009): 149.

about working in a way that enables every member or "partner" to flourish as we seek to reach important goals together.[70]

Lederleitner's book is fresh off the press (2010) and highlights one of the major stumbling blocks to partnership in missions today. Finance is wrapped up in every aspect of partnership from people to projects. It is essential to apply biblical principles to finances and to work out the procedures within each local context.

As the concept of partnership in missions has grown in acceptance around the world, more and more groups are coming up against barriers as they actually try to do it. Some of these issues are revealed in a document that came out of the Philippines. It deals with the basic principles of partnership in missions, which the United Church of Christ collected.[71] I list the first three principles as an example of important issues for them on how to conduct a partnership:

1) The use of the term *partnership* is an attempt by the UCCP to find a new definition of global human relationships!

2) *Partnership* is a covenant relationship entered into by two or more churches sharing common concerns, interests and perspectives based on a mutual recognition and understanding of a common missiological task.

3) *Partnership* implies a reordering of relationships so that historical experiences are transformed into new images of wholeness, mutuality, inter-dependence and unity among covenanting communities.

This document highlights for me that many are struggling with the problem of how to connect with others. They vaguely know they should partner but are constantly being hindered in the areas of equality and unity. This makes me wonder if Christians really understand the theology undergirding the idea of partnership? This is an incentive for this study on a theology of partnership.

---

70. Mary T. Lederleitner, *Cross-Cultural Partnerships: Navigating the Complexities of Money and Mission* (Downers Grove, IL: InterVarsity, 2010), 190.

71. "Basic Principles: A Synthesis Taken from the United Church of Christ in the Philippines Document 'Partnership in Mission,'" *International Review of Mission* 86, no. 342 (July 1997): 339–340, <http://search.ebscohost.com/> (21 June 2010).

Some articles on the "how to" of partnership promoted implementing principles around the globe, even when individual contexts are very different. Douglas Tiessen wrote an article "Global Interdependent Ministry Partnerships in the Russian Context." His desire was to see how more partnership could be accomplished, but he wondered how it works in light of the situation in Russia. Having a large and vibrant church in Russia was part of his context that led to the following statement: "Global interdependent ministry partnerships put the national church in the driver's seat. Too often the nationals of any given country are in the back seat from the outset, which leads to dependency and great difficulty in turning the wheel over to the national."[72] I do not want to doubt in any way the principles gained by Tiessen for the Russian context; they are extremely valuable for that context and for similar contexts. However, in light of this study's context, the principle of putting the national church in the driver's seat is questionable. I am not comfortable with this statement for two reasons. First, context is so important; the CAR is not Russia. What do you do if there is no national church? In the CAR region of the world, believers from a Christian background (rather than believers from the dominant religion background) from nearby nations claim that they are the local church, even though that church is made up of expatriate nationals from outside countries. Second, I am not comfortable with making a blanket policy that says any local church or mission agency or individual should always be put in the driver's seat. That spot is reserved for who ever God chooses. I do, however, understand Tiessen's argument that, historically, missions groups have been slow to see local believers moved into leadership. This needs to be a rigorous part of any strategy: to see new believers raised up in their gifting. They need to be trained, empowered, and released into leadership as soon as possible. But they should not become an island. The new church is part of the whole body of Christ, and there is interconnectedness with the other parts of the body.

Hong-Jung Lee produced an article called "Beyond Partnership, Towards Networking: A Korean Reflection on Partnership in the Web of God's Mission." He states that in the history of mission, the ongoing paradigm change in the development of mission-church relations can be classified

---

72. Douglas P. Tiessen, "Global Interdependent Ministry Partnerships in the Russian Context," *Mission Studies* 22, no. 1 (2005): <ebscohost.com> (21 June 2010), 128.

into four stages: (1) pioneer, (2) parent, (3) partner, and (4) participant.[73] His fourth concept of participation points to the creation of networks. In his view, networks allow the freedom for individuals to reach their maximum potential. He points out that, "Networking indicates people cooperating in interactive and decentralized ways for the accomplishment of some larger purpose."[74] He goes on to say, "Networking is essentially egalitarian with no fixed centre and with no hierarchies, so that its approach can be rigorously horizontal rather than vertical."[75] Having just gone through the process of shifting the CAR Partnership to CAR Network, I think this view makes a lot of sense at the macro level. It brings people to the table as equal players and gives them the ability to create more specific partnerships according to the country, city or project. I like the use of his concept of being rigorous in horizontal relationships; partnerships take effort and time. I would argue, however, that where some type of hierarchy is needed in specific partnerships for a common goal, a rigorous vertical approach is not wasted effort. For example, some projects that include various organizational partners across multiple countries need to have the ability to make decisions that affect the overall good of the project. Because of the multiple players involved, a clear line of communication, authority, and decision making needs to be in place. This takes time and effort to accomplish and have the trust and relationships necessary for the project to move forward.

In conclusion, the "how" of partnership is where the biblical principles come face-to-face with the reality of the specific individuals and contexts involved, as they undertake a common task. Partnerships need structure and vision. They are based on relationships and trust and are geared toward accomplishing agreed goals. Most people know they are supposed to get along and work together. The hard part is to implement biblical truths in local settings where cross-cultural issues muddy the waters. This section on the "how" of partnership has explored the importance of developing trust, accountability, equality, and good financial policies in cross-cultural settings. It has also looked at the particular elements of running a meeting, establishing a joint vision, setting goals, and dealing with conflict resolution.

---

73. Hong-Jung Lee, "Beyond Partnership, Towards Networking: A Korean Reflection on Partnership in the Web of God's Mission," *International Review of Mission* 91, no. 363 (October 2002): <ebscohost.com> (12 June 2010), 577.

74. Ibid., 580.

75. Ibid., 581.

Great skill is needed in moving a group beyond the joint passion of the "why" of partnership to actually being a fruitful, God-pleasing, God-glorifying partnership. Hacket explains, "Partnership, in short, takes will – and skill. It takes the will to persevere forward into the good land of stronger, broader ministry gained only by working together and the skills of successful collaboration to move groups of organizations past the many challenging roadblocks and barriers."[76]

This section on the "how" of partnership has highlighted some of that delicate process. The last question in this literature review takes a look at the potential players who could be involved together in a partnership for the sake of the gospel.

The "Who" of Partnership

This is the final section in the thematic review. It addresses the issue of who potential partners are for partnership activities and what some of the issues hindering partners getting together have been.

A foundational book to the partnership movement is *Partners in the Gospel: The Strategic Role of Partnership in World Evangelization*, with James Kraakevik and Dotsey Welliver serving as editors. In 1991, through the leadership of Phill Butler (Interdev) and James Kraakevik (Billy Graham Center), a working consultation was held to discuss the topic of partnership in world evangelization, and this book was the result. The four areas addressed were: (1) Integrated Partnerships to reach the least evangelized; (2) Church to Church Partnerships, which included Western churches and foreign counterparts; (3) Mission to Mission Partnerships, which included traditional Western agencies, as well as new emerging non-Western agencies; and (4) Two-Thirds-World Partnerships. More than sixty people, coming from five continents and twelve countries, participated in the working consultation. There were forty-eight mission agencies and twelve North American churches represented. The format included presentations on biblical foundations, case studies, and basic principles relating to each of the four major areas. It basically set forth the case for partnership and gave examples of how it is working throughout the world. I believe the significance of the four areas presented is that it demonstrates the potential of who can be involved in

---

76. David Hackett, "Crossing the Will/Skill Divide," Vision Synergy (20 May 2009), <http://www.visionsynergy.net/864/> (5 Aug 2010).

partnership. By kingdom partnerships, I simply mean the universal body of Christ worldwide being potentially available for collaboration on any given goal. Integrated partnerships have the potential to link people from around the world for a specific unreached people group.

A second foundational book is *Working Together with God to Shape the New Millennium: Opportunities & Limitations,* edited by Gary Corwin and Kenneth Mulholland. The book represents the articles and responses presented at the joint IFMA/EFMA/EMS Triennial Conference held in 1999. The theme for the conference was "Working Together to Shape the New Millennium." Some seventeen authors' works are included in the book. Gary Corwin, in his preface, summarizes the content of the book as revealed in the title:

> Namely, that it is God who does the work and that we are privileged to be co-laborers together with Him in all that he is doing. Furthermore, as co-laborers with Him, we are of necessity also co-laborers with all others who belong to Him. Many of our articles focus explicitly on the opportunities and limitations related to that glorious fact.[77]

The book is organized into six sections. Each section contains one or more articles dealing with a specific topic in light of the general conference theme. They include:

- Biblical Foundations for the New Millennium
- The Context of the New Millennium
- Working Together Theologically in the New Millennium
- Working Together Doxologically in the New Millennium
- Working Together Strategically in the New Millennium
- Leadership needed for the New Millennium

Under the theme of the context of the New Millennium, Tom Sine focused on "change" in his article "Setting the Scene for 20/20."[78] Change is coming; we need to make sense of it and plan for it. The future, in his words, must be "taken seriously." There is a need to be proactive instead of reactive to the immense changes surrounding the world. Leaders need to lead with foresight. Globalization, the Internet, connected world financial systems, demographic shifts . . . all add to the massive changes. He concludes,

---

77. Corwin & Mulholland, *Working Together*, 7–8.
78. Ibid., 32.

"There will need to be much more emphasis on new forms of partnership to increase impact and to use limited resources more strategically."[79] I found the articles in this book to be extremely helpful and, at times, challenging. Sine's challenge to understand and use technology is key. The "who" of partnership grows as present technology allows for participation in ways not considered in the past. One example is internet conferencing. People can plan, pray, and fellowship together from almost anywhere in the world.

Most challenging on the issue of "who" in partnership was Edward Rommen's chapter on Orthodox/Evangelical cooperation. He asks the question, "Do you really want to cooperate?"[80] This is a huge issue for ministry in CAR. The majority of church people would come from a non-evangelical background. How do we identify the places where we can partner together? My hope is that by clearly developing a theology of partnership, it would give a starting point for dialogue.

A large number of articles focused on the problems between the "old" churches and the "young" churches or how to form partnerships between the West and the Global South. This is timely, as the Global South is becoming prominent in the region, and the ability to work together and bridge new relationships is strategic. Two representative articles are from Africa and the United States. J. Nelson Jennings wrote an article in the *Presbyterion* titled "Americans and Missions Today." Partnership and networking have become significant options for American churches. He states:

> Particularly in today's ever-changing worldwide Christian scenario, we who are in U.S. local churches must carefully and self-critically determine the roles God wants us to play in world missions. More than simply following a mystical "missionary calling," we must collectively discuss and decide how to follow God's guidance in our missions efforts.[81]

Jennings recognizes the opportunities for global partnerships and that there are unprecedented opportunities where Americans can partner with others in various different ways. There is an attitude of "looking" for partners. Coming from an African perspective was a paper written for a consultation in Yaounde, Cameroon in October 1991, where a desire to partner with churches

---

79. Ibid., 58.
80. Ibid., 139.
81. J. Nelson Jennings, "Americans and Missions Today," *Presbyterion* 33, no. 2 (Fall 2007): <ebscohost.com> (21 June 2010), 84.

from the West is expressed. As the above article focused on what Americans could give in a partnership situation, the Africans want to communicate that they have resources to give to the West, as well. The important point is that partnership goes both ways. Whoever the partners are, it is a two-way blessing. In their report, the Africans plead:

> We urge churches in the north to acknowledge how much they have received from the south in terms of theological and spiritual insights, testimonies, songs and prayers. These non-material gifts probably exceed by far what the north has given to the south in material ones. This exchange should help the churches in Europe and North America to realize the wealth of mutual giving and receiving.[82]

Finally, there is the consideration in the "who" of partnership in the cooperation between local churches and mission agencies. Jerry White addresses this issue in his book, *The Church and the Parachurch: An Uneasy Marriage*. The main purpose of this book is to find a common ground between the local church and what White calls para-local church. The book highlights the tension between the two entities and puts forward some practical suggestions for more understanding and cooperation. The context is the Christian scene in North America, with the myriad of different local churches and para-local church agencies. From a theological perspective, White looks at the doctrine of the local church and the universal church. He examines the Greek word *ekklesia* and its usages in the New Testament. One of the distinctions he brings out is the concept of both the local and mobile parts of the body of Christ. Mobile ministry teams are traced through the book of Acts. He points to Ralph Winter, who sees these missionary teams as a prototype of what is to come, much like the first gatherings of believers were the prototype of local church. The conclusion is that both church and para-local church groups comprise the body of Christ and have a role today.

To summarize the question of "who," partnerships can be formed between individuals, churches, mission agencies or any combination of the above. In today's world, because of technological gains resulting in ease of communication and travel, there are more opportunities for partnership than ever before. Each entity in a partnership is unique, and the level of collaboration for the gospel may vary according to the task and the entities'

---

82. Consultation on "Partnership in Mission – What Structures?" *International Review of Mission* 81, no. 323 (1992): <ebscohost.com> (12 June 2010), 470.

ability to work with others. Between Evangelical and Orthodox entities, a mutual respect and a desire to enter into dialogue is needed. In the case of the West and Global South, an understanding that partnership is a two way street needs to be embraced. Both parties give and receive.

The reality today is that more potential partnership opportunities are available than ever before in history. There needs to be an ethos of a listening ear to the leading of God as he directs ministries, births new ideas, and brings together new partners from around the world to join his purpose, to the praise of his glory. The next section focuses on the different research methods used to approach the topic of partnership.

Methodological Background

The literature revealed several methods of research used in undertaking studies on partnership. Much archival research was used in the gleaning of biblical-theological truths concerning partnership and in documenting the history of past collaborative efforts. Strategic meetings and the ensuing papers from those discussions were also prominent, especially from the WCC and the Lausanne Movement. Lausanne Occasional Papers (LOP) were written in response to discussions on the tensions between the local and universal church in evangelism (LOP #24)[83] and hindrances to partnership (LOP #38).[84] Case studies were widely used in the books of Kraakevik, Butler, and Taylor. In his dissertation, Alvarez combined archival research, participant-observation, and interviews as he examined the ecumenical partnership between two denominations. He set forth the thesis that this was a successful model of a true and mutual partnership.[85]

The promotion and study of partnerships began in earnest in the 1980s. Books, articles, and dissertations began to emerge. An integrated method approach was useful in dealing with partnerships in Christian missions because of the combination of the study of biblical principles and field research.

---

83. "Cooperating in World Evangelization: A Handbook on Church/Para-Church Relationships," *Lausanne Occasional Paper* 24, March 1983, <www.lausanne.org> (2 October 2007).

84. William H. Sunderland and Issue Group No. 9 on Partnership and Collaboration, "Partnership and Collaboration," *Lausanne Occasional Paper (LOP)* No. 38, Pattaya 2004, Copyright 2005, <www.lausanne.org> (2 October 2007).

85. Carmelo Alvarez, "Sharing in God's Mission: The Evangelical Pentecostal Union of Venezuela and the Christian Church (Disciples of Christ) in the United States1960–1980," Dissertation for University of Amsterdam. 10 May 2006, <http://dare.ubvu.vu.nl/handle/1871/9807> (1 September 2009), 8–9.

Integrated research method combines both qualitative and quantitative methods in one study. In his 2007 dissertation on *Cross-Cultural Partnerships Characterized by Grace,* Geoffrey Hahn used both qualitative and quantitative methods. He used archival research to glean biblical principles from Paul on partnership from three specific passages: Ephesians 1:4–10, Corinthians 12, and Ephesians 4:1–6. He then presented the findings in a workshop. Before and after the workshop, he used survey method to determine pre- and post-understanding of partnership.

Several methods have been prominent in partnership research: archival, case studies, surveys, and an integrated research method. A summary follows of what has been gleaned from the literature review and its impact on the direction of this research.

Summary and Research Direction

The idea of strategic partnerships for the gospel became well established in the 1990s and continues to this day. The research reviewed on the subject primarily dealt with practical implementation, such as structure, procedural issues, culture, conflict resolution, and how to run meetings. They all referred to biblical-theological principles of partnership and often referred to the same passages. Unity was a constant theme, as was the body metaphor. Several authors mentioned biblical words and phrases like *koinonia* and *synergo*. In terms of theology, the Trinity and the church local/universal were discussed. All of the biblical-theological issues revealed in the review of the literature were helpful. Five key theological issues emerged that need to be explored in the context of partnership in missions in the CAR. First and foremost is the Trinity. This is the foundation for the other four theological issues and, therefore, partnership itself. The other four issues flow out of the Trinity and are key to informing partnership. They are the purpose of God (*missio Dei*), the body of Christ, the gifts of the Holy Spirit, and the church. There is value in concentrating on these five theological issues, viewing them through the motif of Trinity/relationship and gathering them into one body of work. There needs to be reflection on these theological issues by the constituency of the CARC, thus rooting the research in the CAR context. An integrated method combining archival and survey methods is fitting for this study. The result of this research should build on the platform of existing biblical-theological knowledge and inform toward a theology of partnership in Christian missions in the CAR.

3

Research Design and Methodology

Introduction

This study uses an integrated research approach, which combines the qualitative archival method with the quantitative survey method. According to Creswell, this type of mixing between the two more established methods began around 1959.[1] Also known as the mixed method approach, it involves the collection and analysis of data using both quantitative and qualitative forms in one study. Patton explains:

> Qualitative findings may be presented alone or in combination with quantitative data. Research and evaluation studies employing multiple methods, including combinations of qualitative and quantitative data, are common. At the simplest level, a questionnaire or interview that asks both fixed choice (closed) questions and open-ended questions is an example of how quantitative measurement and qualitative inquiry are often combined.[2]

This integration of data collection methods was necessary for developing a theology of partnership in the CAR, because theological reflection must be done by the author and the community of the CARC. The archival method

---

1. John W. Creswell, *Research Design: Qualitative, Quantitative, and Mixed Methods Approaches* (Thousand Oaks, CA: Sage Publications, 2003), 15.

2. Michael Quinn Patton, *Qualitative Research & Evaluation Methods*, 3rd ed. (Thousand Oaks, CA: Sage Publications, 2002), 5.

sufficed for the study of biblical-theological issues informing partnership, and the survey method allowed the CARC constituency to interact with those issues.

Archival Method

The archival biblical-theological research flows naturally in the qualitative tradition. Creswell explains:

> Writers agree that one undertakes qualitative research in a natural setting where the researcher is an instrument of data collection who gathers words or pictures, analyses them inductively, focuses on the meaning of the participants, and describes a process that is expressive and persuasive in language.[3]

By definition, archival research is dealing with a particular set of existing data and understanding that data; therefore, it is not, in and of itself, concerned with action. It deals with information. This part of the study examined the primary documents of Holy Scripture and sought to inform truths applicable to partnership in Christian missions in the CAR. The journey for this research was deeply rooted in the Bible. As stated earlier by Creswell, qualitative research is inductive by its very nature. This study used the inductive Bible study method. Daniel Sauerwine explains:

> Inductive Bible study is the methodical process that is followed in the study of a biblical passage in order to determine its interpretation from an examination of the data of the text and its context. Inductive Bible study begins with the specific data of the text and moves on that basis toward an interpretation of that text.[4]

Along those same lines, the grammatical-historical method of interpretation was used. R. C. Sproul states:

> Closely related to the analogy of faith and the literal sense of Scripture is the method of interpretation called the grammatico-historical method. As the name suggests, this method focuses attention not only on literary forms but upon grammatical

---

3. Creswell, *Research Design*, 14.

4. Daniel Sauerwein, *Inductive Bible Study: A Proposed Program of Study* (Dissertation DMin for Western Conservative Baptist Seminary, Portland, OR, 1980), 7.

constructions and historical contexts out of which the Scriptures were written.⁵

With the backdrop of the inductive and the grammatical-historical methods, the journey began with the examination of key theological themes. The study commenced with the Trinity, which included the relationship that exists between the three persons of the Godhead and their unique roles as revealed in Scripture in the mission context. The Trinity is foundational to understanding partnership. As revealed in the literature review the Trinity demonstrates unity/diversity, love, community, and relationship. All the other theological issues explored were viewed through the lens of the Trinity. Flowing from this was the examination of the mission of the Triune God. The study moved on to explore the body of Christ. This included its role in the *missio Dei* and its emphasis on relationships, first to the Godhead and then to one another. The gifts of the Holy Spirit were examined in relationship to the Trinity and to the *missio Dei*. Finally, the church (local and universal) was explored in the context of the mission of God.

Survey Method

The purpose of this dissertation is to formulate a theology of partnership in Christian mission in the CAR. In conjunction with the archival research was the field research, of which the survey was the main tool. Theology is not done in a vacuum; it is done in community. It takes into consideration the people who make up the constituency in a given context. Concerning this principle, Paul and Frances Hiebert state:

> Finally, we must test our interpretations within the community of the church. As C. Norman Kraus points out, the Scriptures find meaning and application only within a "community of interpretation." This community includes not only the body of the church living today, but also the saints who have gone before us. It is within this hermeneutical community that other principles of interpretation take their place.⁶

---

5. R. C. Sproul, *Knowing Scripture* (Downers Grove, IL: InterVarsity, 1978), 56.

6. Paul G. Hiebert and Frances F. Hiebert, *Case Studies in Missions* (Grand Rapids, MI: Baker, 1987), 18.

Therefore, there was the need for involvement from the constituency of the CAR. This survey sought that involvement by asking for input on partnership from the people associated with CAR Network (CARN) at their primary gathering point, the yearly CAR Consultation (CARC). This survey was designed to describe CARC attendees' knowledge of biblical-theological principles of partnership, their attitude toward partnership, and their actual participation in the area of partnership. Aaker and Day explain:

> The principal advantage of a survey is that it can collect a great deal of data about an individual respondent at one time. The data may include: (l) depth and extent of *knowledge*; (2) *attitudes*, interests, and opinions; (3) *behavior* – past, present, or intended; and (4) *classification* variables, such as demographic and socioeconomic measures of age, income, occupation, and place of residence.[7]

Arlene Fink described this method as follows:

> A survey is a system for collecting information to describe, compare, or explain knowledge, attitudes, and behavior. Surveys involve setting objectives for information collection, designing research, preparing a reliable and valid data collection instrument, administering and scoring the instrument, analyzing data, and reporting the results.[8]

The results of the survey gave insight into the present knowledge, attitude, and behavior of the CARC attendees, which related specifically to partnership in the CAR.

The design process for the survey contained the following elements: the population, the objectives of the survey, the survey mode, the survey questionnaire, the pre-test, the analysis plan, and the reporting of the results.

Population

Glass and Stanley describe two types of statistics: descriptive and inferential. Inferential refers to taking a sample set of data and, through it, inferring the properties of a larger set. This survey, however, deals with the first, which they

---

7. David A. Aaker and George S. Day, *Marketing Research*, 2nd ed. (New York: John Wiley & Sons, 1983), 135.

8. Arlene Fink, *The Survey Handbook* (Thousand Oaks, CA: Sage Publications, 1995), 1.

define as follows, "*Descriptive statistics* involves the tabulating, depicting, and describing of collections of data. These data may be either quantitative, such as measures of height and weight, or qualitative, such as sex and personality type."[9] The aim of this survey is to describe the responses of only one group of people – those who are in attendance at the 2009 CARC. There is no projection intended to any other or larger group. Two hundred seventeen of the two hundred thirty attendees at the consultation returned a survey. Twelve of the surveys were incomplete and were excluded from the results. Therefore, the CARC Survey results consisted of data from two hundred five surveys.

Survey Objectives

In order to do theology in community, interaction with the CARN community is necessary. The archival studies have produced information on the five theological issues, and the need is to discover how the CARN constituency sees these issues from their perspective. One needs to know their knowledge, attitude, and behavior on each theological issue. The knowledge is divided into two parts, objective and subjective. The objective part is to know if they are familiar with the theological issue. For example, do they agree that the Trinity is Father, Son, and Spirit? The subjective part of knowledge would then be how they apply this specific truth. Following from the responses on knowledge, there is the need to know what the respondents' attitudes are towards partnership in the context of the five theological issues. Finally, there is the need to know the respondents' behavior in the context of partnership.

The objective of the survey is to provide the information on the five theological issues from the perspective of the CARC attendees. This will help in the theologizing process and will inform a theology of partnership in Christian mission in the CAR. The data needed is outlined in the "Information Needs Matrix" in Table 1.

---

9. Gene V. Glass and Julian C. Stanley, *Statistical Methods in Education and Psychology* (Englewood Cliffs, NJ: Prentice-Hall, 1970), 2.

Table 1: Information Needs Matrix

Information Type / Theological Theme	Objective Knowledge	Subjective Knowledge	Attitude	Behavior
The Trinity	Are respondents familiar with biblical teaching on Trinity?	Do respondents recognize any implications of Trinity teachings for partnership?	Does the Trinity inspire partnership in this context?	Does this generate partnership behavior?
God's Mission	Are respondents familiar with biblical teaching on God's Mission?	Do respondents perceive implications of these teachings for partnership in mission?	Does God's mission inspire partnership in this context?	Does this generate partnership behavior?
The Body of Christ	Are respondents familiar with biblical teaching on body of Christ?	Do respondents recognize any implications of these teachings for partnership in mission?	Does the body of Christ inspire partnership in this context?	Does this generate partnership behavior?
God's Gifts	Are respondents familiar with biblical teaching on spiritual gifting?	Do respondents perceive implications of these teachings for partnership in mission?	Does the spiritual gifting inspire partnership in this context?	Does this generate partnership behavior?
Church Local/ Universal	Are respondents familiar with biblical teaching on local/universal church?	Do respondents perceive implications of these teachings for partnership in mission?	Does the local/universal church inspire partnership in this context?	Does this generate partnership behavior?

Survey Mode and Questionnaire

The survey mode was a self-administered questionnaire, using closed questions with ordinal responses, with one open-ended question. The survey questionnaire was composed of three parts: an introduction, the main body of questions/statements, and the classification data questions. The main body of the survey questions followed the "information needs" matrix but was presented in a mixed-up order. The survey concluded with an open-ended question, which allowed the respondents to voice whatever they considered important concerning partnership. The questionnaire was designed to be as brief as possible so that it could be completed within ten to fifteen minutes. It was created to be simple and easy to navigate, even for English-as-a-second-language respondents.

Pretest

Before the implementation of the survey, a test-run was undertaken. "The purpose of such pretests is to find out how the data collection protocols and the survey instruments work under realistic conditions."[10] The pretest contained the review of questions for content, the review of questions for clarity, and the implementation of the test survey. This process included two separate groups. The first was the review group. They were chosen because they are specialists who understand partnership and have experience in survey development. They reviewed both the content and clarity of presentation of the questions. They made sure that all the relevant questions were being asked and all questions fit the objectives. They also helped to ensure that the language used was clear and simple.

The second group was the international test group. Because the attendees of the CARC are from multiple countries, cultures, and languages, it was important to run a pretest of the potential questions to check for clarity. After the review group gave input into the survey, it was then given to the International test group, made up of people from Egypt, Switzerland, and the Netherlands. They were asked to take the entire survey and to give feedback on the clarity of the introduction and instructions, the clarity of the questions, and the total ease of the survey experience. Their input was then incorporated into the final survey.

---

10. Floyd J. Fowler, *Survey Research Methods,* 3rd ed. (Thousand Oaks, CA: Sage Publications, 2002), 112.

Analysis Plan

The survey was administered at the November 2009 CARC, which was held in a CAR city. The surveys were numbered, distributed, and collected by volunteers. The margin of error for the survey was in the recording process. Therefore, the surveys were tallied twice to insure the correctness of the recording of the data. A seven-point Likert scale was used. For the demographic section, each of the responses was given a numerical identity. If a question was left blank, then it was assigned a numerical identity, as well, to represent the fact that it was left blank. The data was grouped according to the two most common measures of central tendency used with the Likert scale: the median, and the mode.

Reporting of Results

The results of the survey will be made available to anyone who would like them from within the CARN. No names were recorded on the questionnaires to insure privacy. The results were distributed within the CARN Council, which is the governing structure within the CAR Network.

Summary

In order to inform on a missiological theology of partnership in the CAR, integrated research was undertaken. Qualitative archival research was conducted on five theological issues, which are the Trinity, the Purpose of God, the Body, the Gifts, and the Church. A quantitative survey was undertaken with the attendees of the 2009 CARC. The survey described the interaction of the CARC attendees with the five theological issues in the three areas of knowledge, attitude, and behavior as they relate to partnership in the CAR.

4

Partnership and the Trinity

Introduction

The purpose of this chapter is to examine the Holy Trinity in terms of being the foundation for work and relationships in Christian missions today. The Trinity is the starting point and the lens through which to view the topic of partnership in Christian missions. This section will begin with an introduction to the doctrine. It will proceed to examine three aspects of the Trinity: the distinct roles of the Three-in-One, how the persons of the Godhead relate to one another, and examples of the One-in-Three working on behalf of mankind. The findings will be briefly summarized at the end of the chapter.

The Trinity: An Overview

God is one! This is the clear cry of the Old Testament. It is found in the *Shema*, the prayer recited each morning by Jews and taken from Deuteronomy 6:4–6: "Hear, O Israel: The LORD our God, the LORD is one. Love the LORD your God with all your heart and with all your soul and with all your strength. These commandments that I give you today are to be upon your hearts." This was the cry for hundreds of years, and the Lord Jesus reiterated it while being challenged by a teacher of the Law. "What is the greatest commandment?" he was asked. He responded "The most important one is this: 'Hear, O Israel, the Lord our God, the Lord is one." (Mark 12:29). This has been the creed of Jews and Christians since the beginning. Over time, God, in his sovereignty, has chosen to reveal to his creation the depth, beauty and mystery of this Oneness.

The Oneness of God is the beginning point. The complexity of this Oneness is revealed in three basic, yet eternally profound, words: "God is love," ὁ θεὸς ἀγάπη ἐστίν (1 John 4:8, 16). Every evangelical believer knows this. Sometimes the familiar loses its depth and wonder. This simple phrase is often only highlighted in terms of God's love for mankind as revealed in Christ's death on the cross. "God is love" reveals more than the atoning work of Christ; it reveals who God is. God never changes. God has always been "love." God is love before the creation of man, before the creation of the world. Therein lies a foundational truth. How can there be "love" unless there is community? God from eternity past is love. Love exists within the Godhead. It is the One-in-Three and Three-in-One, which dwells in community, that "is love." It is this foundational truth, which the Godhead itself has chosen to reveal to mankind, that highlights the importance of relationship. The Catholic theologian Leonardo Boff reflects, "In the beginning is not the solitude of a One, of an eternal Being, alone and infinite. Rather, in the beginning is the communion of the three Unique Ones. Community is the deepest and most foundational reality that exists."[1] To delve into the depths of the Trinity, one quickly discovers that at the core of the Godhead is relationship. The reality of this relationship permeates all that is revealed in the Scriptures, from Genesis to Revelation. To summarize, Darrell Johnson states, "What does it all mean? It means that in the deepest mystery of his being God is an intimate relationship, a fellowship, a community of love."[2]

This love relationship is demonstrated in statements between God the Father and God the Son. "And a voice from heaven said, 'This is my Son, whom I love; with him I am well pleased'" (Matt 3:17). The Father's love for the Son is also stated in Matthew 17:5; Mark 9:7; Luke 9:35; 2 Peter 1:17; and John 3:35. The Son's love for the Father is proclaimed in John 14:31, "but the world must learn that I love the Father and that I do exactly what my Father has commanded me."

The One-in-Three is displayed clearly in four triadic passages. The first is seen in the words of Jesus as he addresses the disciples in Matthew 28:19–20 "Therefore go and make disciples of all nations, baptizing them in the name of the Father and of the Son and of the Holy Spirit, and teaching them to obey everything I have commanded you. And surely I am with you always,

---

1. Leonardo Boff, *Holy Trinity, Perfect Community* (Maryknoll, NY: Orbis, 2000), 4.

2. Darrell W. Johnson, *Experiencing the Trinity* (Vancouver, BC: Regent College Publishing, 2002), 51.

to the very end of the age." To highlight the concept of the One-in-Three, "the name" (τὸ ὄνομα) in verse 19 is singular. It is "the name" of the three Persons. The second is found in the words of Paul, as he gives the benediction to the Saints in Corinth: "May the grace of the Lord Jesus Christ, and the love of God, and the fellowship of the Holy Spirit be with you all" (2 Cor 13:14). Third, again in Paul's writings, we read of his words to the church in Thessalonica:

> But we ought always to thank God for you, brothers loved by the Lord, because from the beginning God chose you to be saved through the sanctifying work of the Spirit and through belief in the truth. He called you to this through our gospel, that you might share in the glory of our Lord Jesus Christ. (2 Thess 2:13–14)

Finally, the writer to the Hebrews states, "How much more, then, will the blood of Christ, who through the eternal Spirit offered himself unblemished to God, cleanse our consciences from acts that lead to death, so that we may serve the living God!" (Heb 9:14).

It is not the purpose of this chapter to outline the proofs for the deity of the distinct Persons of the Godhead or the proof of the Oneness of the Three. Rather, it is to accept this as revealed truth and move on to explore the relationship between the persons of the Godhead, the distinct roles revealed for each, and the way the Holy Trinity works as one.

Orthodox evangelical belief states that each member of the Godhead is in essence identical, and each person is distinct. Bruce Ware expounds:

> It affirms that the Father, Son, and Holy Spirit each possesses the divine nature *equally*, so as to avoid Arianism; *eternally*, so as to avoid thinking of God's nature as created; *simultaneously*, so as to avoid modalism; and *fully*, so as to avoid any tri-partite understanding of the Trinity (e.g. like a pie divided into three equal pieces). The Father, Son, and Holy Spirit are not each one-third God, but each is fully God, equally God, and this is true eternally and simultaneously.[3]

In addition to the introduction above, Robert Letham, in his book *The Holy Trinity*, lists five vital parameters concerning the discussion of the Trinity that are helpful for this study:

---

3. Bruce A. Ware, *Father, Son, & Holy Spirit Relationships, Roles, & Relevance* (Wheaton, IL: Crossway, 2005), 41.

1) One being – three persons; three persons – one being.
2) The three persons are *homoousios*.
3) The three persons mutually indwell one another in a dynamic communion.
4) The three persons are irreducibly different from one another.
5) There is an order (*taxis*) among the persons.

Louis Berkhof, in his *Systematic Theology*, lists six:

1) There is in the divine Being but one indivisible essence (*ousia, essentia*).
2) In this one divine Being, there are three persons or individual subsistences: Father, Son, and Holy Spirit.
3) The whole undivided essence of God belongs equally to each of the three persons.
4) The subsistence and operation of the three persons in the divine Being is marked by a certain definite order.
5) There are certain personal attributes by which the three persons are distinguished.
6) The church confesses the Trinity to be a mystery beyond the comprehension of man.

The above descriptions of the Triune God are represented well in Darrell Johnson's diagram seen in Chart A.[4]

---

4. Darrell Johnson, *Experiencing the Trinity*, 46.

Chart A: The Triune God

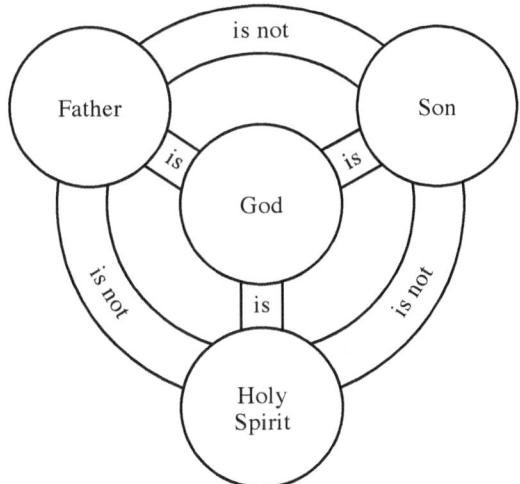

The understanding and development of the doctrine of the Trinity took hundreds of years. As the church grew and various men began to promote their view of the Father, Son, and Holy Spirit, great debates and councils were held. Creeds were created to address the errant views that contradicted the biblical revelation. "Modalism" was founded by Sabellius in the third century AD. In trying to understand the relationship between the persons of the Godhead, this view held that the Father was God, the Son was God, and the Spirit was God. However, this happened successively. The one God took on different "modes" to reveal himself. God was not simultaneously Father, Son, and Spirit.

A second renowned person was a priest from Alexandria Egypt, Arius, who lived in the early fourth century. Arius wanted to preserve the idea that there is One God and only One God. In his zeal, he claimed that Christ, while to be honored, was merely the first and greatest creation of the One God. This belief became known as "Arianism." He gained many followers, and eventually there was a church council held in Nicea in AD 325 where this very issue was addressed. Athanasius, Arius' former Bishop, led the charge proclaiming that Christ was indeed God the Son and of the same nature (*homoousios*) as the Father. As a result of this council, Arius was condemned and exiled, and a creed was produced called the creed of Nicea.[5] The result of the council was

---

5. Creed of Nicea, http://www.thenagain.info/webchron/Mediterranean/ConstanChrist2.html, (5 March 2009).

the clear statement of the deity of the Lord Jesus. To firmly establish the deity of the Holy Spirit, another council was held in Constantinople in the year AD 381.

> Here, the heroes were the Cappadocian Fathers, whose names were Basil, Gregory of Nyssa, and Gregory of Nazianzus. These three courageous theologians defended the Spirit's deity, and in the end, the council of Constantinople expanded the Nicene creed to affirm that the Holy Spirit, the Lord and Life-Giver, proceeds from the Father and is to be worshiped with the Father and the Son.[6]

Historically, another major concern for the church on the issue of the Persons of the Trinity was the *"Filioque* clause." This clause stated that the Spirit proceeds from the Father and the Son. The dispute over this clause was one of the major reasons for the split between the Eastern and the Western church. Letham traces the adoption of the clause in the West:

> However, in Spain, due to the threat of a continued Arianism, in localized liturgies an addition crept in – a *patre filioque* – "from the Father and the Son." This addition of *filioque* spread and was adopted by local councils, particularly the Council of Toledo (589), and was accepted by the French church in the late eighth century, but was not inserted into the Creed by Rome until 1014 under Pope Benedict VIII. The Fourth Lateran Council of 1215 mentioned it, and the Council of Lyons in 1274 proclaimed it as dogma.[7]

In conclusion, God is one; God is love; the Three-in-One dwells in complete harmony, distinct in persons and one in essence. There is order in the Triune Godhead, and there are distinct personal attributes. This knowledge of the One-in-Three has been revealed to man through the Holy Scriptures by the Godhead itself and has been affirmed by the church over the centuries. The doctrine of the Trinity and its development over the years is an important starting point. Helpful to the discussion of partnership is the examination of the unity of the Trinity and the relationship between the three Persons of the Godhead, which is the topic of the next section. The issues of

---

6. Ware, *Father, Son, & Holy Spirit*, 39.

7. Robert Letham, *The Holy Trinity in Scripture, History, Theology, and Worship* (Phillipsburg, NJ: P & R Publishing, 2004), 202.

unity and relationship are central to how partnerships should work and the Trinity serves as the ultimate model. The next section explores these issues.

The Trinity: Unity and Relationship

The Eternal Godhead, One-in-Three and Three-in-One, for eternity past has been in relationship in a communion of holiness. The love between the Persons of the Trinity is expressed in many ways throughout Scripture. Ware writes:

> God's tri-Personal reality is intrinsic to his existence as the one God who alone is God. He is a socially related being within himself. In this tri-Personal relationship the three Persons love one another, support one another, assist one another, team with one another, honor one another, communicate with one another, and in everything respect and enjoy one another.[8]

Particularly in the West, this focus on the relationship between the persons of the Godhead has not received much attention. Yet, it is this glimpse into the characteristics of the Living God that should instruct all of our relationships in how we see ourselves, how we see others, and how we interact together in the body of Christ. In his systematic theology, Shedd lists at least twelve ways in which the Holy Trinity is described as relating together:[9]

1) One person loves another (John 3:35)

2) Persons dwell in one another (John 14:10, 11)

3) One person suffers for another (Zach 13:7)

4) One person knows another (Matt 11:27)

5) Persons address one another (Heb 1:8)

6) One person is the way to another (John 14:6)

7) One person speaks of another (Luke 3:22)

8) One person glorifies another (John 17:5)

9) The persons confer with one another (Gen 1:26; 11:7)

---

8. Ware, *Father, Son, & Holy Spirit*, 21.

9. William G. T. Shedd, *Dogmatic Theology*, 2nd ed. (Nashville, TN: Thomas Nelson, reprinted 1980), 279.

10) The persons make plans with one another (Isa 9:6)

11) One person sends another (Gen 16:7; John 14:26)

12) One person rewards another (Phil 2:5–11; Heb 2:9)

In addition to the wonderful expressions of relationship listed above by Shedd, there are three others that carry weight in the Scriptures as relating to the Godhead. They are unity, joy, and peace.

Unity

Probably the greatest passage on unity in the Scripture is found in Christ's high priestly prayer in John 17. The unity between the Father and the Son is total, and the desire to draw mankind into that unity is striking in its grace. Jesus begins in verse twenty: "My prayer is not for them alone. I pray also for those who will believe in me through their message, that all of them may be one, Father, just as you are in me and I am in you. May they also be in us so that the world may believe that you have sent me." He continues in verse 23: "I in them and you in me. May they be brought to complete unity to let the world know that you sent me and have loved them even as you have loved me." This same unity is expressed in Ephesians 4:3 as being the unity of the Spirit. This characteristic of unity is not only central to the Godhead but it is vital for witness. Christ mentions twice that it is by the world seeing this unity that they will know he comes from the Father. There is continual harmony and unity amongst the Three-in-One.

Joy

Joy is a hallmark of the Trinity and of the kingdom of the Trinity. Jesus was full of joy (John 15:11; 17:13). Life in the Spirit is joy, as Romans 14:17 states: "For the kingdom of God is not a matter of eating and drinking, but of righteousness, peace and joy in the Holy Spirit." Again, in John 15:13, we see the dual working of the Father and Spirit: "May the God of hope fill you with all joy and peace as you trust in him, so that you may overflow with hope by the power of the Holy Spirit." Jesus, for the joy fixed before him, endured the cross (Heb 12:2). God rejoices over his people (Zeph 3:7). A characteristic of the Godhead is this gladness to be together in communion. Joy is found in being in relationship. It is found in the midst of abundant love. The Three Persons are found together expressing joy in Luke 10:21: "At that time Jesus, full of joy through the Holy Spirit, said, 'I praise you, Father, Lord of heaven and earth, because you have hidden these things from the wise and learned, and revealed them to little children. Yes, Father, for this was your good pleasure.'" There is unrestrained pleasure and joy within the Godhead as they relate to one another and to their creation.

Peace

God the Father is characterized by peace (1 Cor 14:33; Rom 15:33). God the Son is characterized by peace (1 Cor 1:3; Eph 1:2; John 14:27; Col 3:15). God the Spirit is characterized by peace (Rom 8:6; Gal 5:22). Many letters of the New Testament begin with a greeting of peace to the readers. Peace is communicated in many benedictions, as well. Paul tells the Thessalonians, "Now may the Lord of peace himself give you peace at all times and in every way. The Lord be with all of you" (2 Thess 3:16). Peace is freedom from anxiety and inner turmoil. It is freedom from worry. It represents tranquility. The Godhead is characterized by peace. It is a reflection of the sovereignty and all-encompassing nature of the Three-in-One.

In conclusion, Scripture discloses that the Persons of the Trinity love one another, honor one another, give glory to one another, dwell in one another, confer with one another, and make plans with one another. Their relationship and essence is characterized by joy, unity and peace. Those who strive to work together in partnership have a model in the Godhead, a standard that has been revealed to man because God would have Believers strive for this type of relationship and unity as they live and work together. Having focused on the unity and relationship between the Three Persons, we move on to examine the diversity within that unity. Unity does not mean uniformity, and within partnerships there needs to be a celebration of the different roles that individuals bring to the task.

The Trinity: Diversity in Roles

God is both One-in-Three and Three-in-One. In this section, the "Three" will be examined. The Triune God has chosen to reveal glimmers of truth in Scripture that emphasize the working and Persons of the Trinity. Bruce Ware states, "The three Persons of the Godhead exhibit distinct roles in relation to one another. Distinct tasks and activities in accomplishing their common plan characterize nearly all of the work that the true and living God undertakes."[10]

The most prominent revelation of roles revealed in Scripture is in the Father-Son role of the first two Persons of the Trinity. It is God Almighty who desires to reveal himself with the name "Father." It is his idea and plan. The name "Father" is used hundreds of times throughout the Bible. In the Gospel of John, chapters 14–16, "Father" appears forty-four times! In relation to God the Father, Holy Scripture also reveals Jesus as "God the Son." He is referred to as "Son" over forty times in the Gospel of John alone. Jesus is called the "only begotten son" or "the one and only son" (John 3:16; 18:1:14, 18). Jesus is called the "Son of God" (ὁ υἱὸς τοῦ θεοῦ) (John 1:49; 3:18; 11:27; 19:7; 20:31). Most revealing is that Jesus calls himself the Son of God in John 5:25, 10:36, and 11:4. He claims ". . . what about the one whom the Father set apart as his very own and sent into the world? Why then do you accuse me of blasphemy because I said, 'I am God's Son'?" (John 10:36). Throughout the New Testament, the Father-Son description is used. This distinction is also demonstrated in heaven after the death and resurrection of Jesus. Revelation 2:18 reads: "To the angel of the church in Thyatira write: These are the words of the Son of God, whose eyes are like blazing fire and whose feet are like burnished bronze." In another passage, the Son of God is described as the Lamb in connection with God the Father; the Father is seated on his throne and the Lamb on his right side (Rev 5:6, 13).

The Scriptures clearly show a distinction between the Father and the Son. In the following paragraphs, the Father, then the Son, and then the Holy Spirit will be looked at in closer detail to highlight the roles that specifically apply to them in the Godhead.

God the Father

The designation "Father" reveals his role within the Trinity. In speaking of the relationship between the Father and the Son in the Gospel of John, Köstenberger and Swain explain, "The Father enjoys personal priority in the *taxis* (order) of the triune life, not ontological superiority, for the Father and the Son hold all things in common: one divine name (17: 11), one divine

---

10. Ware, *Father, Son, & Holy Spirit*, 20.

power (5:19, 21–22), one divine identity (10:30)."[11] The Father is the one who is revealed as being seated on the throne in heaven (Ps 93:2; 103:19; Isa 66:1; Matt 23:22; Rev 5). He is the one who is supreme among the Persons of the Godhead (Ps 2:2; 1 Cor 15:28). The Father is the grand architect that oversees the fulfilling of his purposes. "And he made known to us the mystery of his will according to his good pleasure, which he purposed in Christ, to be put into effect when the times will have reached their fulfillment to bring all things in heaven and on earth together under one head, even Christ" (Eph 1:9–10). Every good and perfect gift comes down from the Father. He is the originator and giver (Jas 1:17). In this role as giver of gifts, the Father is shown as the one who gave the ultimate gift. He gave his only Son for the world (John 3:16). This is also brought to light in Romans 8:31–32, "What, then, shall we say in response to this? If God is for us, who can be against us? He who did not spare his own Son, but gave him up for us all – how will he not also, along with him, graciously give us all things?" It is Christ who opens up the way for a reconciled relationship with the Father (2 Cor 5:18–19). It is Christ who told mankind to call God "Father" (Matt 6:9). It is to the Father that we pray and bring our requests. Finally, it is the Father who will wipe away every tear, and believers will dwell with him:

> And I heard a loud voice from the throne saying, "Now the dwelling of God is with men, and he will live with them. They will be his people, and God himself will be with them and be their God. He will wipe every tear from their eyes. There will be no more death or mourning or crying or pain, for the old order of things has passed away." (Rev 21:3–4)

God the Son

Jesus Christ is revealed as the Eternal Word. The prologue to the Gospel of John sets the scene for the entire gospel, where the Father-Son picture is so prominent. In the first few verses of John, the Word is revealed as being God. "In the beginning was the Word, and the Word was with God, and the Word was God. He was with God in the beginning" (John 1:1–2). In commenting on this verse, Köstenberger and Swain say, "According to John, the Word, while distinct from God, is at the same time intrinsic to his own identity: it

---

11. Andreas J. Köstenberger and Scott R. Swain, *Father, Son, Spirit: The Trinity and John's Gospel* (Downers Grove, IL: InterVarsity, 2008), 123.

existed with God 'in the beginning.'"[12] The Father has sent the Son, and the Son has a very distinct role on the earth. It is Jesus who emptied himself and became a part of the human race. Paul proclaims this incarnation in his letter to the Philippians:

> Who, being in very nature God, did not consider equality with God something to be grasped, but made himself nothing, taking the very nature of a servant, being made in human likeness. And being found in appearance as a man, he humbled himself and became obedient to death – even death on a cross! (Phil 2:6–8)

Jesus became the Lamb. John the Baptist shouted, "Look, the Lamb of God, who takes away the sin of the world!" (John 1:29). He remains the Lamb in heaven, where he receives praise for this role. "In a loud voice they sang: 'Worthy is the Lamb, who was slain, to receive power and wealth and wisdom and strength and honor and glory and praise!'" (Rev 5:12).

Jesus was the one who became human in order to destroy the work of the devil. "Since the children have flesh and blood, he too shared in their humanity so that by his death he might destroy him who holds the power of death – that is, the devil (Heb 2:14). Also, it says in 1 John 3:8, ". . . The reason the Son of God appeared was to destroy the devil's work."

Jesus' role was to do the will of the Father and to do the Father's works. Over and over, Jesus made it clear that he came in obedience to the Father and to do the Father's will (John 5:30, 36; 6:38–40; 8:16–18, 26, 49). Jesus explained his submission to the Father. His obedience was central to his role and to his relationship with his Father. Paul tells the Corinthians that the head of Christ is God in 1 Corinthians 11:3. The level of submission is seen in John 8:28–29, where Christ says that he "does nothing on his own" and that "I always do what pleases him." In John 14:31 Jesus says that the world must learn that he does exactly what the Father says. The ultimate act of obedience and submission to the Father was his acquiescence to being beaten, scourged, and nailed to a cross. "Submission" in today's world seems politically incorrect; within the Godhead, it is cherished. In today's world, "submission" reeks of hierarchy; it says that one part is better and higher than the other. This is not the case in the Godhead. Ware explains:

> There is an ordering in the Godhead, a "built-in" structure of authority and submission that marks a significant respect in

---

12. Köstenberger and Swain, *Father, Son, Spirit*, 43.

which the Persons of the Godhead are distinguished from one another. Surely, they are not distinct in essence, for each shares fully the identically same divine nature. Their distinction, rather, is constituted, in part, by *taxis* – the ordering of Father, Son, and Holy Spirit within the Godhead. The order is not random or arbitrary; it is not Spirit first, Son second, and Father third, nor is it any way other than the one way that the early church, reflecting Scripture itself (Matt 28:19), insisted on: Father, Son, and Holy Spirit.[13]

Christ's obedience to the Father was in line with another purpose. It was to reveal the Father to the people of the world. To see Jesus and to know Jesus was to know the Father (John 17:26). Philip wanted to know the Father. He asked Jesus to show him the Father. "Philip said, 'Lord, show us the Father and that will be enough for us.' Jesus answered: 'Don't you know me, Philip, even after I have been among you such a long time? Anyone who has seen me has seen the Father. How can you say, "Show us the Father"?'" (John 14:8–9).

Another role of Christ is to build the church. We see that the Father "placed all things under his feet and appointed him to be head over everything for the church, which is his body, the fullness of him who fills everything in every way" (Eph 1:22–23). Jesus himself makes the claim in Mark 16:18, where he tells Peter, "I will build my church and the gates of hell will not prevail against it."

God the Spirit

The Third Person of the Trinity, God the Spirit, has several different names revealed just within the Gospel of John. He is called the "Spirit of Truth" τὸ πνεῦμα τῆς ἀληθείας (John 14:17; 15:26), the "Holy Spirit" τὸ πνεῦμα τὸ ἅγιον (John 14:26; 20:22), and the "Counselor" (helping presence) παράκλητος (John 14:16, 26; 15:26; 16:7). In examining the role of the Holy Spirit, Ware writes:

> Not only does the Spirit reveal and inspire the *word of Christ*, and empower the proclamation of the *gospel of Christ*, and regenerate sinners to behold the *beauty of Christ*, and lead us to place our

---

13. Ware, *Father, Son, & Holy Spirit*, 72.

hope and *faith in Christ*, the Spirit also works mightily in us to conform us more and more into the *likeness of Christ*.[14]

This statement succinctly summarizes some of the major roles of the Holy Spirit. We see that the Holy Spirit is the One who inspires the authors of the Scriptures. "Above all, you must understand that no prophecy of Scripture came about by the prophet's own interpretation. For prophecy never had its origin in the will of man, but men spoke from God as they were carried along by the Holy Spirit" (2 Pet 1:20–21).

The role of the Holy Spirit is described in the work of men's hearts in several different ways. It is the Spirit who "will convict the world of guilt in regard to sin and righteousness and judgment" (John 16:8). The Spirit is the one who speaks, teaches, and leads believers (Acts13:2, Acts 10:19–20). "But the Counselor, the Holy Spirit, whom the Father will send in my name, will teach you all things and will remind you of everything I have said to you" (John 14:26). It is the Spirit who fills and seals believers in Christ: "And do not grieve the Holy Spirit of God, with whom you were sealed for the day of redemption" (Eph 4:30). It is the Holy Spirit that empowers God's people to do the work of evangelism: "But you will receive power when the Holy Spirit comes on you; and you will be my witnesses in Jerusalem, and in all Judea and Samaria, and to the ends of the earth" (Acts 1:8). It is the Holy Spirit that imparts spiritual gifts to the body of Christ. This role is one of the most profoundly apparent in the lives of the people of God today.

> Now to each one the manifestation of the Spirit is given for the common good. To one there is given through the Spirit the message of wisdom, to another the message of knowledge by means of the same Spirit, to another faith by the same Spirit, to another gifts of healing by that one Spirit, to another distinguishing between spirits, to another speaking in different kinds of tongues, and to still another the interpretation of tongues. All these are the work of one and the same Spirit, and he gives them to each one, just as he determines. (1 Cor 12:7–11)

The Role of the Holy Spirit was central to the life of Christ on Earth. The Spirit overcame Mary while she was yet a virgin (Luke 1:35). The Holy Spirit filled Jesus in the Jordan at baptism and then led him into the wilderness

---

14. Ibid., 122.

(Luke 4:1). The Spirit was on Jesus as he went about his public ministry (Luke 4:18–19).

There is one last aspect of the role of the Holy Trinity to be considered here. It is the fact that the Holy Spirit never takes the spotlight. The Holy Spirit is always pointing to the Father and the Son, always giving glory and honor to the Father and the Son, and never to himself. The Spirit makes known the Son and the Father and is the "background" power for much of what the Godhead does. ". . . the Holy Spirit's new covenant ministry in all its distinctive aspects is essentially to glorify Christ to us and in us and through us and to cause us consciously to live in and from our relationship to him as our Saviour, Lord, and God."[15]

In conclusion, the Father's role is revealed as the grand architect. He holds primary position in the *taxis* of the Trinity. He is revealed as seated on the throne in heaven and the one who is in control of history, sending the Son and the Spirit. He is the giver of every good gift from above and will be the one in heaven to wipe away every tear at the consummation. The role of the Son brings to light the plan of God in the power of the Spirit. Jesus is revealed as the living Word. He is God incarnate. He came to be the sacrificial lamb and die on the cross to redeem men to God. He lived in complete obedience and submission to the Father. He destroyed the works of the devil, and he is the one presently building his church. The Role of the Spirit is seen to be an empowering one. The Holy Spirit empowered Jesus on Earth, his disciples after him, and the church today. The Spirit inspired the authors of the Scriptures and imparts spiritual gifts to individuals. He continues to teach and guide believers and to convict the world of sin. The Holy Spirit always points to and gives glory to the Father and the Son.

The examination of the distinct roles within the Trinity has demonstrated that diversity within unity makes for a rich community. This is a good example for those involved in partnerships, as they learn to honor different roles and those who represent them. There does not need to be competition. When each role flows in the power of God, the unified whole becomes a blessing. The next section joins unity, diversity, and action as different works of the Triune God are examined.

---

15. J. I. Packer, *Keep in Step with the Spirit* (Old Tappan, NJ: Fleming H. Revell, 1984), 164.

The Trinity: Together in Action

When the story of God in the Holy Bible is read through the lens of the Trinity, the screen changes from black-and-white to color with surround sound. The interconnectedness of the Godhead is revealed in many events and divine acts on behalf of a lost world. From the very beginning, in Genesis, this divine partnership of the One-in-Three is involved in the creation story. "As St Augustine put it, the world was made by the Father, through the Son, in the Holy Spirit. Each Person stamps creation with something of its own specific property. That is why creation is so rich, because behind it and within it is hidden the wealth of each divine Person, as that Persons is, ever distinct and ever in communion."[16]

As the biblical story unfolds, major works of the Triune God, such as redemption and salvation, are seen to be works where the Persons of the Godhead are intricately involved together in achieving the end result. This is displayed in the salvation story, where the Father sends the Son. The Spirit fills and guides the Son. The Son embraces the cross and, through his death and resurrection, enables the reconciliation between God and man. Another example is seen in the creation of the church. Christ is the head, appointed by the Father. The Holy Spirit imparts gifts to the body of Christ for the work of mission for the Father. The distinct Persons of the Godhead work in their unique way to fulfill the purpose of the Triune God. This is revealed in the prayer of the Apostle Paul on behalf of the Ephesians:

> For this reason I kneel before the Father, from whom his whole family in heaven and on earth derives its name. I pray that out of his glorious riches he may strengthen you with power through his Spirit in your inner being, so that Christ may dwell in your hearts through faith. And I pray that you, being rooted and established in love, may have power, together with all the saints, to grasp how wide and long and high and deep is the love of Christ, and to know this love that surpasses knowledge – that you may be filled to the measure of all the fullness of God." (Eph 3:14–19)

Table 2 highlights different works of God and how Scripture describes the participation of the Persons in the Godhead.

---

16. Boff, *Holy Trinity*, 104.

Table 2: Participation of the Persons in the Godhead

Work	Verse	Person
Creation	Gen 1:2; Ps 33:6b; Job 33:4	Spirit
	John 1:3; Col 1:15f; Heb 1:1–4	Jesus
	1 Cor 8:6	Jesus & Father
	Gen 1:1;	God
	Gen 1:26	Trinity
Salvation	Exod 15:2; Ps 13:5; John 3:16–17; Acts 28:28	Father
	Heb 9:14	Jesus & Spirit
	Acts 4:12; Eph 1:13; 1 Thess 5:9; 2 Tim 2:10	Jesus
Redemption	Isa 43:1; 44:22; Luke 1:68	Father
	Rom 3:24; Gal 3:13; 4:5	Jesus
	Rom 8:23; Eph 4:30	Spirit
	1 Cor 1:30; Eph 1:7	Father & Jesus
Sanctification	Eph 3:14–19	Trinity
	Rom 15:16; 2 Thess 2:13	Spirit
	1 Cor 6:11	Jesus & Spirit
	John 17:19; 1 Cor 1:2	Jesus
	1 Thess 4:3	Father
Mission	Matt 28:18f	Trinity
	John 20:21	Father & Jesus
	Acts 1:8	Spirit
Indwelling	John 14:13	Father & Son
	Rom 8:9; John 3:6	Spirit

The above table lists multiple works of God and the specific involvement of the Persons of the Trinity in each specific work. It is a beautifully intertwined tapestry of love and unity. As Ware states, "We have seen over and again that what one member of the Trinity does affects another. The interconnectedness and interdependence among the members of the Trinity is such that one is hard pressed to think of any 'work of God' which does not involve various members of the Trinity working together."[17]

---

17. Ware, *Father, Son, & Holy Spirit*, 134.

Summary and Reflection

In summary, God has revealed himself to mankind as the One-in-Three. God from eternity past has existed in perfect community, in perfect love, and perfect relationship. The three persons of the Godhead are equal, of the same divine essence, totally one in their unity and totally distinct in their persons. There is complete unity and diversity. There is a *taxis* beginning with the Father, Son, and Holy Spirit. This is demonstrated in their roles. The Father is the grand architect. The Son is the Lamb of God, the Word that became flesh. The Spirit is the one who indwells, empowers and guides. The One-in-Three is revealed as working together in creation and salvation. The relationship within the Godhead is marked by love, purpose, unity, joy, and peace.

In reflection, the concept of the Trinity had not been in the forefront of my thinking, either for myself or for the ministry of the CAR Partnership. The most haunting comment from the reading was the question, "What does 'God is love' mean before the creation of man?" That continues to grab my attention two years after reading it. My theological motif was christological. The ideas of community and rejoicing in others were also side issues for me. We had a job to do – to reach all the lost in the CAR. People were paying a high cost for this missionary work – prison, deportations, sickness, etc. The thought of pausing and taking joy in fellow workers for no other reason than they were part of God's community was a new experience. The Godhead is so in love with one another and with their creation. I confess that I did not see fellow workers in the CAR through God's eyes. My relationship with them was based on what they could do or what we could do together. This fresh look at the Trinity has given a new paradigm for me for what a partnership should be. At the core should be community, love, and relationship. The partnership is an extension, for however long it exists, of being in Christ and part of his body. May God help me to view each person, young or old, experienced or fresh, as he does, with value for who they are as God's child, made in his image. May I rejoice as he does in their presence and fellowship. May I go beyond "task" to cherish and pursue the individual.

The study of the Holy Trinity has laid the first blocks of the foundation in building towards a theology of partnership in Christian missions. This foundation is based on love, relationship, roles, order, unity, diversity, purpose, joy, and peace. The ethos of partnership lies in these qualities and characteristics. The following chapter builds upon this foundation by examining the purpose of God, the *missio Dei*. God is on the move in history, and he has chosen to include his people in his great mission.

5

Partnership and the Purpose of God

Introduction

This chapter focuses on relationship. It examines the relationship between God and his creation, man. It reveals how that relationship was destroyed and then restored. It begins with the fall and proceeds with a glimpse of the future reconciled state in heaven, which centers on community, love, and dwelling face-to-face with God. It examines the cost of reconciliation through the death of Christ, the sending of the Holy Spirit to indwell and guide his church, and God's invitation to his people to join him in his mission of reconciling the world to himself. This chapter takes a look at the grand plan of God as revealed throughout the Bible. His purpose of restoring the broken relationship with mankind, resulting in paradise restored, is the first section. The following sections demonstrate how God's purposes are fulfilled through the coming of God the Son and the Holy Spirit. Throughout all, God's purposes are seen to be in partnership with those who love him.

God's Overall Purpose

God has revealed himself as the eternal One-in-Three. He has a deep love for his creation (mankind) and a deep desire for fellowship with man. He has demonstrated this through divine revelation, which is found in the Holy Scriptures. This, in and of itself, is a testimony to God's desire to reach out to mankind. The fact that Scripture exists, a result of God inspiring human authors to reveal hidden secrets from heaven, demonstrates his desire for relationship with mankind and that he is the one who initiates it. Christopher Wright brings out this point, quoting Charles Taber:

> The very existence of the Bible is incontrovertible evidence of the God who refused to forsake his rebellious creation, who refused to give up, who was and is determined to redeem and restore fallen creation to his original design for it. . . . The very existence of such a collection of writings testifies to a God who breaks through to human beings, who disclosed himself to them, who will not leave them unilluminated in their darkness, . . . who takes the initiative in re-establishing broken relationships with us.[1]

The purpose of God or *missio Dei* is all about fulfilling his mission in the world. It is "concerned with nothing less than the completion of all that God has begun to do in the creation of the world and of humankind."[2] It is a grand scheme that seeks, once and for all, to redeem and reconcile man to God. The outworking plan includes partnering with men like Abraham, Moses, and David. It finds its enabling authority in the death and resurrection of Christ. It continues on to this day through the presence and empowering of the Holy Spirit in the body of Christ. The church has been reconciled to God and commissioned to be his ambassador to a lost world with the message of reconciliation (2 Cor 5:19).

The story of the relationship between the Godhead and man begins in the book of Genesis. The Triune God of eternity past forms the universe, the world, and mankind.

Creation

He did not have to, but he did. God created the heavens and the earth. He created mankind. The Godhead spread their arms and embraced this new community. God's awesome power and glory are revealed in what he made. He did it by speaking his word. "Let all the earth fear the LORD; let all the people of the world revere him. For he spoke, and it came to be; he commanded, and it stood firm" (Ps 33:8–9). Much of the creation story deals with nature, but, for the purpose of this study, it is man that is the focus. God's

---

1. Christopher Wright, *Mission of God*, 48.
2. Lesslie Newbigin, *The Open Secret: An Introduction to the Theology of Missions* (Grand Rapids, MI: Eerdmans, 1978), 56.

delight in his creation is recorded along the way; after each day, he expresses that "it was good" (Gen 1:4, 10, 12, 18, 21, 25). In Genesis 1:26 the account of Man's creation is reported. The Godhead decreed, "Let us make man in our image, in our likeness." Man was different. He was made in God's likeness and image. He was ordained to rule over the animals. Yet, God saw that man was alone. There was no other creature comparable to Adam. God determined to make a companion for him (Gen 2:18). God's priority on the importance of relationship came to the fore. The first earthly relationship was instituted, and it would reflect unity and diversity. "The man said, 'This is now bone of my bones and flesh of my flesh; she shall be called "woman," for she was taken out of man.' For this reason a man will leave his father and mother and be united to his wife, and they will become one flesh" (Gen 2:23–24). Thus, the first couple of the world began life in the Garden of Eden, in the presence of the living God, where they knew him face-to-face (Gen 3:8–10).

The world was perfect. Adam and Eve were perfect. However, this paradise was not to last.

The Fall

When God created all things in the beginning, he declared them to be very good (Gen 1:3). He created man in his image to be in relationship with himself and one another. Concerning this state, Newbigin writes:

> The human in the Bible exists only in relationship with other persons and only as part of the created world. In both the creation stories of Genesis these two points are insisted upon. Humanity exists only in the double form of man and woman. The image of God is present in this relatedness-in-love (Gen 1:27). And it is immediately added that "God blessed them and said to them: 'Be fruitful and multiply and fill the earth and subdue it'" (1:28). Human life from its beginning is a life of shared relationship in the context of a task – a task that is continuous with God's creative work in the natural world.[3]

In Genesis 3 the disobedience and fall of man is recorded. God had strictly forbidden the eating of fruit from the tree in the middle of the garden; the result, if they did, meant death (Gen 3:3). Eve was deceived by the serpent and

---

3. Ibid., 69.

ate. Adam soon followed, and their disobedience and rebellion birthed sin in them and, consequently, in all who would be born of their seed. "Therefore, just as sin entered the world through one man, and death through sin, and in this way death came to all men, because all sinned" (Rom 5:12).

For Adam and Eve, this was the end of paradise. All that they had known (which was very good) was soon to change. Glasser explains:

> As a result, a death process began in Adam and Eve, a sickening that would eventuate in their physical death ("to dust you will return," 3:19). This tendency would corrupt and disrupt their relationships with God (3:10), between man and woman (3:12), between Cain and Able (4:8), and with the environment (3:17–19).[4]

Sin was born. J. Oliver Buswell defines sin as, "anything in the creature which does not express, or which is contrary to, the holy character of the Creator."[5] The major consequence of the fall was banishment from the garden. The new state of reality was that Adam and Eve were no longer welcome in the presence of God. Their relationship was broken. Isaiah 59:2 says: "But your iniquities have separated you from your God; your sins have hidden his face from you, so that he will not hear." Derek Kidner, in his commentary on Genesis, writes: "The expulsion is by decree; it could also be expressed as by logical necessity, since eternal life is fellowship with God (John 17:3), which man has now repudiated."[6]

The design of the eternal Godhead for community and fellowship with man was now impossible. God, holy and righteous in his character, sent them away from his presence. The road back to community in his presence would be long and costly. This mission, God's mission, is what the Bible is about from Genesis 1 to Revelation 22. The end result will be a restored relationship in the future eternal state.

---

4. Arthur F. Glasser, *Announcing the Kingdom: The Story of God's Mission in the Bible* (Grand Rapids, MI: Baker, 2003), 40–41.

5. Carl F. H. Henry, ed. *Basic Christian Doctrines: Contemporary Evangelical Thought* (Grand Rapids, MI: Baker, 1962), 104–105.

6. Derek Kidner, *Genesis: An Introduction & Commentary* (Downers Grove, IL: InterVarsity, 1967), 72.

The Future State

One of the great privileges of having the Holy Bible is the ability to see the grand plan of God, from beginning to end as it concerns mankind, and live in the middle of the story. It is easy to open the pages of the book of Revelation, peek into the future, and discover how the story ends. Understanding the end of the story and the focus of scripture on God's love and relationship with mankind teaches us now what is eternally important and impacts how we live our lives.

Creation Restored

What was started in the book of Genesis is completed in the book of Revelation. God created a paradise, a community that was polluted through sin. In the eternal state to come, these will be restored. In *Announcing the Kingdom,* Glasser gives a list comparing what is and what is to come:[7]

1) Paradise lost	Paradise regained
2) Creation of heaven and earth	A new heaven and a new earth
3) Tree of life Guarded	Tree of life restored
4) Communion destroyed	Communion restored
5) Work cursed	Work blessed
6) People out of harmony with nature	People at peace with nature

Two specific passages, Revelation 21:1–6 and Revelation 22:2–4, will be looked at to gain a fuller understanding of the consummation of God's purpose as it pertains to mankind. He declares that he will be with them and that they will see him face-to-face.

> Then I saw a new heaven and a new earth, for the first heaven and the first earth had passed away, and there was no longer any sea. I saw the Holy City, the new Jerusalem, coming down out of heaven from God, prepared as a bride beautifully dressed for her husband. And I heard a loud voice from the throne saying, "Now the dwelling of God is with men, and he will live with them. They will be his people, and God himself will be with them and be their God. He will wipe every tear from their eyes. There will be no more death or mourning or crying or pain, for the old order

---

7. Glasser, *Announcing the Kingdom*, 361.

of things has passed away." He who was seated on the throne said, "I am making everything new!" Then he said, "Write this down, for these words are trustworthy and true." He said to me: "It is done. I am the Alpha and the Omega, the Beginning and the End. To him who is thirsty I will give to drink without cost from the spring of the water of life." (Rev 21:1–6)

In the previous chapter on the Trinity, the core concepts of love, community, and fellowship were revealed. John the seer presents a future eternal state where these three core concepts again are central. Reflecting on the appearance of the eternal city, Mounce states:

> The vision itself takes the form of a magnificent city descending from heaven. It symbolizes the eternal felicity of all who follow the Lamb. Kiddle writes that the heart of the symbol is a community of men: "It is a city which is a family. The ideal of perfect community, unrealized on earth because of the curse of sin which vitiated the first creation, is now embodied in the redeemed from all nations" (pp. 415–416). Hunter writes, "The consummation of the Christian hope is supremely social. It is no 'flight of the alone to the Alone' but life in the redeemed community of heaven." The holy city (cf. Isa 52:1; Matt 4:5) is of heavenly origin. It comes down from God, that is to say, the church is not a voluntary organization created by man but a fellowship initiated and given by God (cf. Matt 16:18).[8]

Verse 3 punctuates the love God has for man and his desire to live in fellowship with his creation. This has been his message throughout the Old and New Testaments. It is a loud voice from the throne that pronounces three times in one short verse that God will dwell *with* them and live *with* them and be *with* them. Mounce points out the significance of the words "dwell" (σκηνή) and "live" (σκηνώσει).

> A great voice is heard out of the throne, announcing the fulfillment of a basic theme that runs throughout the OT. It is clearly stated in the Holiness Code of Leviticus 26, "I will make my abode with you . . . and will be your God, and you shall be my people" (Lev 26:11–12; cf. Jer 31:33; Ezek 37:27; Zech 8:8).

---

8. Robert H. Mounce, *The Book Of Revelation* (Grand Rapids, MI: Eerdmans, 1977), 370–371.

The voice from heaven declares that the tabernacle of God is with men and that he shall dwell with them. The Greek word for tabernacle (*skene*) is closely related to the Hebrew *Shekinah*, which was used to denote the presence and glory of God. In the wilderness wanderings the tabernacle or tent was a symbol of the abiding presence of God in the midst of his people. In the fourth Gospel, John writes that the Word became flesh and tabernacled (*eskenosen*) among men so that they beheld his glory, glory as of the only Son from the Father (John 1:14). When the Seer writes that the tabernacle of God is with men, he is saying that God in his glorious presence has come to dwell with man. The metaphor does not suggest a temporary dwelling. From this point on God remains with his people throughout eternity.[9]

In verse 4, the tender heart of the Father is revealed as he personally wipes away every tear from their eyes. It demonstrates his understanding of his children's sufferings, pains and tribulations. He is not a God who is far away and distant. It reveals his tenderness, concern and love.

Finally, in verse 6, the announcement "It is done" is in the context of his restored relationship and community. Literally Γέγοναν is a perfect tense and has the meaning "they are come to pass." Dana and Mantey explain the implication of the use of this tense: "The perfect is the tense of complete action. Its basal significance is the progress of an act or state to a point of culmination and the existence of its finished results."[10] God has fulfilled all his purposes and, as a result, forever and ever a community now exists that lives in perfect love and in his very presence. Hughes summarizes:

> The announcement made by the great voice from the throne now heard by St. John is, in effect, the announcement of the fulfillment of all God's covenant promises; for the central message of these promises is that God's presence and dwelling will be with mankind in a relationship of perfect and joyful harmony between the creator and his creatures.[11]

---

9. Ibid., 371–372.

10. H. E. Dana and Julius R. Mantey, *A Manual Grammar of the Greek New Testament* (Toronto, Canada: Macmillan, 1927), 200.

11. Philip Edgcumbe Hughes, *The Book of the Revelation: A Commentary* (Leicester: IVP, 1990), 223.

This passage revealed the new heaven and the new earth with God's presence with man. John continues with the revelation in the next chapter.

> No longer will there be any curse. The throne of God and of the Lamb will be in the city, and his servants will serve him. They will see his face, and his name will be on their foreheads. (Rev 22:3–4)

The Father and the Son (Lamb) are mentioned together sharing the throne, ὁ θρόνος τοῦ θεοῦ καὶ τοῦ ἀρνίου. "Throne" is singular. The location of the throne is in the midst of the people, who will serve and worship the Father and the Son. Thus, they will be in the physical presence of Almighty God. No one has seen the Father except the Son (John 6:46), but in the new eternity there is no separation. Hughes explains:

> To see his face indicates a personal relationship of absolute trust and openness. This is confirmed by the assertion that his name will be on their foreheads (see comments above on 3:12; 7:3; 14:1), for this signifies not only their preciousness to him, to whom they gladly belong (cf. 1 Cor 6:19f.) but also that in the multitude of the redeemed who populate the holy city there will be none who are unknown and unloved, none whose identity is lost in the crowd, and none who miss seeing him face to face.[12]

One last note coming from the grand picture of Revelation is the people of God being called the "bride" of Christ. This special designation highlights the relationship between Christ and his church. It also highlights the joining of the church with the Spirit in the *missio Dei*. It becomes a foundational principle that undergirds collaboration.

The Bride of Christ

We have seen above the direct relationship between God the Father and his loved ones, and now we see the relationship of the Lord Jesus, the Lamb who was slain for our sins, receiving us as his bride to the wedding party. "Let us rejoice and be glad and give him glory! For the wedding of the Lamb has come, and his bride has made herself ready" (Rev 19:7). Again, in Revelation 21:9 the description is "I will show you the bride, the wife of the Lamb." Beyond the intimacy revealed here between Christ and his people are the oneness and unity expressed in the term "bride," as it refers to all those who are saved. There are multitudes of people and yet one bride. There is a unique

---

12. Ibid., 233.

relationship between individuals within the body of Christ. They are one and seen as one by the Father and the Son. In a final thought about the bride, there is a challenge given within the last few verses of the book of Revelation. There is a strong invitation to come to God, found in Revelation 22:17: "The Spirit and the bride say, 'Come!' And let him who hears say, 'Come!' Whoever is thirsty, let him come; and whoever wishes, let him take the free gift of the water of life." Three times the present middle imperative "come" (Ερχομαι) is used. The present tense indicates the open invitation to the reader. It is a call to come to God, and, in light of the content of the book of Revelation, to come before it is too late and history comes to a close and the eternal state begins. The middle voice "refers back the action to the acting subject."[13] The call to come is issued by two parties: the Spirit and the bride. They are seen to be working together on behalf of mankind in the church age. Glasser writes:

> That the Holy Spirit and the church in union should beseech men and women to be reconciled to God, and that this should be virtually the final word addressed to the human race in Holy Scripture is most significant. It points up what Charles Van Engen has defined as a new word for defining the essence of the church: a deep "yearning" to gather all peoples around the cross and around the throne of the Lamb and into its unity, its holiness, its catholicity, its apostolicity, and its witness.[14]

The final state of those who are followers of Christ and witnesses of the consummation of God's purposes in response to the fall has been explored. It is time to briefly highlight the outworking of God's purpose that fills the pages between Genesis and Revelation. To his glory and our praise, God has chosen to restore creation and mankind to himself through Christ. As revealed in Scripture, the end result is a restored relationship: God dwelling with man face-to-face. Love, relationship and community are the eternal results and, therefore, highlight their priority for believers today. This eternal state hints to how people should live and work together today. The final verses in Revelation invite mankind to come to Christ: the Spirit and the bride say come. Displayed here is the partnership between God and his people in the proclamation and accomplishment of the purposes of God. All throughout Scriptures, God has reached out to his servants and invited them to join

---

13. Dana & Mantey, *Manual Grammar*, 157.
14. Glasser, *Announcing the Kingdom*, 373.

with him in his great mission. The next chapter explores how God's plan was unfolded and the role of his people in it.

God's Purpose in the Old Testament

Returning to the Garden of Eden in Genesis chapter 3, God confronts his creation. Even while pronouncing judgment on the Serpent, a glimmer of hope is promised and a seed of victory proclaimed. Addressing the serpent, God discloses, "And I will put enmity between you and the woman, and between your offspring and hers; he will crush your head, and you will strike his heel" (Gen 3:15). This verse demonstrates God's power, authority, and control over the future. Kidner explains, "There is good New Testament authority for seeing here the *protevangelium*, the first glimmer of the gospel."[15] God's plan is already in motion. His purpose will be to glorify himself, reverse the destructive work of the Devil, and restore the broken relationship between man and himself.

Key to the Old Testament is the implementation of covenants. Grudem defines covenant as, "an unchangeable, divinely imposed legal agreement between God and man that stipulates the conditions of their relationship."[16] Covenants were an integral part of ancient society. They were made between individuals, tribes or royal houses. Each covenant was unique, spelling out the terms, promises, and stipulations. It was through covenants that the people of this time were able to expand relationships. This is the background meaning to the Hebrew word *berit*.[17] This is the concept God chose to use for Abraham, the people of Israel, and David. It was familiar to them and allowed them to enter into a special partnership with the living God.

Abraham

God's unfolding purpose is revealed slowly over thousands of years. A major step forward in the implementation of his plan was the way he dealt with Abraham. "I will make you into a great nation and I will bless you; I will make your name great, and you will be a blessing. I will bless those who bless you,

---

15. Kidner, *Genesis*, 70.

16. Grudem, *Systematic Theology*, 515.

17. R. Laid Harris, Gleason L. Archer, and Bruce K. Waltke, *Theological Wordbook of the Old Testament* (Chicago, IL: Moody Press, 1980), 129.

and whoever curses you I will curse; and all peoples on earth will be blessed through you" (Gen 12:2–3). This covenant with Abraham demonstrates God's sovereignty in overseeing his purpose. Glasser states, "The salvation of the nations was God's ultimate motivation in making Abraham's name great and in being the God of Abraham's innumerable progeny. This universal purpose totally dominates the covenant."[18] Another aspect of the Abrahamic covenant is that it strongly exposes God's desire to partner with mankind in the accomplishment of his plan. A relationship is being formed for the glory of God and the outworking of history. Moses, in talking to the children of Israel, proclaimed the deep love of God for Abraham and those who were to follow: "To the LORD your God belong the heavens, even the highest heavens, the earth and everything in it. Yet the LORD set his affection on your forefathers and loved them, and he chose you, their descendants, above all the nations, as it is today" (Deut 10:14–15). God set his affections on the forefathers. The word used is *chashaq*. It has the meaning of:

> a deep inward attachment (in a positive sense) . . . In the case of emotions (to which the biblical usage is limited) it is that love which is already bound to its object. It should be distinguished from *ahav* which means love.[19]

In several places Abraham's special relationship with God is revealed in the word "love" (*ahav* in the Hebrew.) It is translated "friend" by the NIV. In the Old Testament, King Jehoshaphat, when addressing God, referred to "Abraham your friend." More impressive is Isaiah 41:8, where God himself declares, "But you, O Israel, my servant, Jacob, whom I have chosen, you descendants of Abraham my friend." There is also one verse in the New Testament. James, speaking of Abraham, says, ". . . he was called God's friend" (Jas 2:23). The word used by James for friend is φίλος which Louw and Nida define as, "a male person with whom one associates and for whom there is affection or personal regard – 'friend.'"[20] Several commentators, including D. E. Hiebert, point to the dialogue between Abraham and God in Genesis 18 concerning the destruction of Sodom and Gomorrah. Should God hide from him what he is about to do or confide in him? God chooses to confide in him, and then, in a very Middle Eastern way, the bargaining starts for the

---

18. Glasser, *Announcing the Kingdom*, 59.
19. Harris, Archer, and Waltke, *Theological Wordbook*, 773.
20. Johannes P. Louw and Eugene A. Nida, eds. *Greek-English Lexicon of the New Testament Based on Semantic Domains* (New York: United Bible Societies, 1988, 2nd ed. 1989).

lives of people. The picture revealed here is that, "God regarded and treated Abraham as an intimate friend, one who understood and entered into the divine purposes."[21]

The mission of God unfolded further as God intervened in history and delivered the Jewish people from bondage in Egypt. His purpose was to demonstrate his power, deliver them, and enter into a partnership with them for the sake of the rest of the world.

The People of Israel

The Exodus of the Jews from Egypt is ripe with significance, as it demonstrates the awesome grace and saving power of God. The institution of the Passover, with its image of the shedding of blood for the salvation from holy judgment, is a type of the ultimate sacrifice that is to come in Christ. Now a nation, God takes the next step in his progression by announcing the purpose of this nation for the world:

> You yourselves have seen what I did to Egypt, and how I carried you on eagles' wings and brought you to myself. Now if you obey me fully and keep my covenant, then out of all nations you will be my treasured possession. Although the whole earth is mine, you will be for me a kingdom of priests and a holy nation. (Exod 19:4–6)

God delivers the Israelites, and then he brings them to himself. This completes the sacrificial type, as the power of God destroys the enemy, covering the people with blood to avoid death in order to bring the people to himself. The result of this covenant with Israel is that God has appointed a nation of people to be priests. The role of priest was two-fold: to bring the knowledge of God to the rest of the Israelites and to bring the sacrifices of the people to God. Within this, they were to bless the people. God has chosen, at this point of history, to partner with an entire nation. It is a nation that he has chosen, that he has set apart and dedicated to service. The service was to be priests for a lost world. Wright states, "As the people of YHWH they would have the historical task of bringing the knowledge of God to the nations, and bringing the nations to the means of atonement with God."[22]

---

21. D. Edmond Hiebert, *The Epistle of James: Tests of a Living Faith* (Chicago, IL: Moody Press, 1979), 196.

22. Christopher Wright, *Mission of God*, 331.

God continued his partnership with mankind in accomplishing his mission through his special relationship with King David. Through David, he points to the ultimate King who will come.

David

God continued his covenantal relationships with King David. In rejecting Saul, God declared his desire for a man that would be after his own heart: "But now your kingdom will not endure; the LORD has sought out a man after his own heart and appointed him leader of his people" (1 Sam 13:14). Wright points out that in Hebrew the heart is the seat of the will and intentions, and the intention of this phrase is that David will be the one who will carry out the purposes of God.[23] The New Testament confirms this in Acts 13:22, "After removing Saul, he made David their king. He testified concerning him: 'I have found David son of Jesse a man after my own heart; he will do everything I want him to do.'" God promised to David that his kingdom, his house, his line, and his throne would last forever (2 Sam 7:16; Ps 89:4). All of this was to be fulfilled in the coming of Jesus as the Son of David.

God is sovereign. He is orchestrating history, and he is moving towards the consummation of all his purposes. Each individual believer is caught up in this journey. It is God's journey. He is seeking to use his people in partnership with him along the way. This is an important concept for Christians to grasp; believers are part of a bigger whole, and they need to see themselves and those around them in that light. As more of God's unfolding purpose is revealed in Scripture, we see that the Lord Jesus Christ is the realization of all the covenants and promises of the Old Testament. He is the crescendo to which the thirty-nine books of the Old Testament have been building. The next section examines the coming of Christ and the Holy Spirit and their importance to the *missio Dei*.

God's Purpose in the New Testament

The purpose of the Triune God, in restoring the relationship with man, takes a gargantuan step forward in the incarnation of God the Son. This action of love reverses the curse of sin and allows for the reconciliation of man with God. The sending of the Spirit seals the believers and initiates them into

---

23. Ibid., 344.

the family of God, where they become part of the Godhead's ministry of reconciling the rest of the world to himself.

The Son of God

The Gospel of John states forty-three times, in different ways, that God the Father *sent* the son. One example is found in John 5:30, "By myself I can do nothing; I judge only as I hear, and my judgment is just, for I seek not to please myself but him who sent me." It is through Jesus that the ultimate purpose of God is fulfilled. Jesus opened the door for the reconciliation between God and man. There is much to learn from the "sentness" of Jesus. The verse above hinted at the relationship between the Father and the Son in this mission.

The following insight contributes to the thoroughness of the relationship as an example for all who will follow in Jesus' footsteps. Lois Fuller quotes Kostenberg and O'Brien:

> The sent one is to know the sender intimately (7:29; cf. 15:21; 17:8, 25); live in a close relationship with the sender (8:16, 18, 29; 16:32); bring glory and honour to the sender (5:23; 7:18); do the sender's will (4:34; 5:30 ,38; 6:38–39) and works (5:36; 9:4); speak the sender's words (3:34; 7:16; 12:49; 14:10b, 24); follow the sender's example (13:16); be accountable to the sender (many places; compare esp. ch. 17); bear witness to the sender (12:44–45; 13:20; 15:18, 25); and exercise delegated authority (5:21–22, 27; 13:3; 17:2; 20:23).[24]

The Father and the Son, one in essence, unique in their roles, begin the work necessary for the salvation of mankind.

The Word, which was with God, became flesh and dwelt with men. He came with a set mission to accomplish. He destroyed the work of Satan, and he redeemed and reconciled mankind.

The Devil's Work Destroyed

The conflict concerning man began with the serpent in the Garden of Eden but was finished with Jesus on the cross. Jesus came to crush the work of Satan, reverse the curse, and restore the ability for man to be in the presence of God. John writes, "He who does what is sinful is of the devil, because the devil has

---

24. Lois K. Fuller, *A Biblical Theology of Missions: God's Great Project for the Blessing of All Nations* (Bukuru, Nigeria: African Christian Textbooks, 2005), 85.

been sinning from the beginning. The reason the Son of God appeared was to destroy the devil's work" (1 John 3:8). This was accomplished through the atoning work of the cross. Christ took on himself the punishment mankind deserved. God's holiness and justice were satisfied, and his love, grace, and mercy were poured out. Christ's victory on the cross resulted in two major gains for man: redemption and reconciliation.

Redemption

Christ came to redeem mankind from sin. There was no other way, and God the Father, in his love and sovereignty, made the costly payment for the restoration of man. Concerning the need for redemption:

> Whenever men by their own fault or through some superior power have come under the control of someone else, and have lost their freedom to implement their will and decisions, and when their own resources are inadequate to deal with that other power, they can regain their freedom only by he intervention of a third party. In the NT, depending on the aspect envisaged, the Gk word-groups associated with *lyo*, to free (42 times in NT) is used to express liberation from bonds or by payment of a ransom (*lytron*).[25]

English words like "redeem" (λυτρόω), "ransom" (λυτρον, αντιλυτρον), which emphasize the means or instrument by which the release is acquired, and "redemption" (λυτρωσις ἀπολύτρωσις) all focus on the payment of a price for release. In classical Greek it was used in reference to slaves who had been captured in a war; a ransom was paid for them that they might attain their freedom. God has redeemed believers from the horrible judgment to come. With redemption comes the forgiveness of sins. The apostle Paul states, "In him we have redemption through his blood, the forgiveness of sins, in accordance with the riches of God's grace" (Eph 1:7).

Reconciliation

The concept that relates most directly to this study is that of reconciliation. It points back to the foundational issues of love, relationship, and community found in the Trinity and revealed to be the ethos of heaven. It is the answer

---

25. Colin Brown, *The New International Dictionary of New Testament Theology*, Vol. III (Grand Rapids, MI: Zondervan, 1971), 177.

to the separation established through the sin in Genesis 3. It also reflects the purpose of God to bring all men to himself.

In his letter to the Romans, Paul rejoices, "For if, when we were God's enemies, we were reconciled to him through the death of his Son, how much more, having been reconciled, shall we be saved through his life! Not only is this so, but we also rejoice in God through our Lord Jesus Christ, through whom we have now received reconciliation" (Rom 5:10–11). The word "reconciled" used here is the verb καταλλάσσω. The noun form is καταλλαγή. It means to re-establish proper, friendly, interpersonal relations after these have been disrupted or broken.[26] Another form of this root word, ἀποκαταλλάσσω, is found in Colossians 1:19–20. Here Paul says, "For God was pleased to have all his fullness dwell in him, and through him to reconcile to himself all things, whether things on earth or things in heaven, by making peace through his blood, shed on the cross" (Col 1:19–20). A touching aspect of this verse is the idea that the Father was pleased with Christ. The word "pleased" is εὐδοκέω. It is also found in Matthew 3:17, declaring the Father's pleasure in the Son at his baptism. Bruce adds, "It was God's good pleasure, moreover, to reconcile all things to himself through Christ."[27] There is a delight, a joy in the Father in the ministry of reconciliation. He wants the relationship and community with mankind restored. It is not done grudgingly.

In 2 Corinthians 5:18–19, there is one more aspect to the message of reconciliation found: "All this is from God, who reconciled us to himself through Christ and gave us the ministry of reconciliation: that God was reconciling the world to himself in Christ, not counting men's sins against them. And he has committed to us the message of reconciliation." God is calling on his people to partner with him in this tremendous message. He wants his people to share in the joy of the message and the results of the message. This leads to the last section of this chapter, which is the mobilization of God's people through the enabling of the Holy Spirit.

The Holy Spirit

Both the Father and the Son sent the Holy Spirit (John 14:26; 16:7). Today the Holy Spirit is the one leading, guiding, counseling, rebuking, enabling, and

---

26. Louw and Nida, *Greek-English Lexicon*.
27. F. F. Bruce, *The Epistles to the Colossians, to Philemon, and to the Ephesians* (Grand Rapids, MI: Eerdmans, 1984), 74.

empowering the people of God for the glory of God and the advancement of his ultimate purpose. The disciples were told to wait: "Do not leave Jerusalem, but wait for the gift my Father promised, which you have heard me speak about" (Acts 1:4). Jesus went on to instruct, "But you will receive power when the Holy Spirit comes on you; and you will be my witnesses in Jerusalem, and in all Judea and Samaria, and to the ends of the earth" (Acts 1:8).

The Spirit came on Pentecost, and the church age was birthed. The Spirit immediately put people on the move, sending Phillip to the Ethiopian Eunuch (Acts 8:29), Peter to Cornelius (Acts 10:44–47), and the first missionary team to Cyprus (Acts 13:2). Glasser summarizes:

> With the advent of the Holy Spirit on the day of Pentecost, God's redemptive activity shifted from working through a particular people (the descendants of Abraham via Isaac and Jacob and Israel) to working in the midst of all peoples. On that day the New Testament expression of the people of God, the church, was formed and empowered for its worldwide mission. This marks the resumption of universal history with which the Bible begins. (Gen 1–11)[28]

Summary and Reflection

The Triune God exists in a relationship of love and unity. God, in his sovereignty and wisdom, created the world and mankind to rule it. He had great pleasure in the creation, and he made man in his image. They met face-to-face and enjoyed community in the Garden of Eden. The Fall changed all of that, and, as a result, Adam and Eve were banished from the Garden and separated from God. The land was cursed, and sin was born. Thus begins the great narrative of the purpose of God. God's desire is to see the broken relationship restored and all things brought together under the headship of his Son. Revelation reveals the completion of God's purpose: man is restored to a face-to-face relationship with God, and they dwell together for eternity. From Genesis to Revelation, the plan of God unfolds. This plan includes partnership with mankind, whom he created in his image. God chose to work with Abraham, who was called his friend. The plan grew to a partnership with a nation, who he called to be his chosen people. He chose David to point

---

28. Glasser, *Announcing the Kingdom*, 259.

the way to the coming Messiah. After the death and resurrection of Jesus, the partnership rose to a whole new level, as the Father and the Son sent the Holy Spirit to indwell and to lead the church. God is now partnering with the worldwide body of Christ. From beginning to end, God has included people in his grand purpose. He has called them to be a part. He has called them to join the Godhead in the reconciliation of man to himself. This group of people is given instructions not only on "what" to do but "how" to do it.

In reflection, God is sovereign, and yet we get so caught up in our plans, our strategies, and our agendas for CAR Consultations. Where is the fear, the respect, the awesome awareness of our God? Where is the quiet reflection and joint submission as a community? We have grasped that we are partners with God. We act like we are the senior partners. Looking back over the years, some of the most precious CARC moments were the times of sharing the Lord's Supper, the times when people shared what the Holy Spirit had taught them, when people had bowed together in prayer and worship, often with tears. God loves the nationals more than any of us love them. He will accomplish his purposes. We need to be careful to acknowledge this truth in our attitudes and actions as we plan and create programs and projects in CAR. We need to pursue God together, not just talk about him. Part of pursuing God together means pursuing one another. This takes time, effort and sacrifice. God's revealed purpose is reconciliation. Heaven is described as a place with perfect relationship. This must be a major component of who we are as a community as we join God in his purpose for CAR.

This chapter has focused on the purpose of God in reconciling the world to himself. It emphasized that he has chosen to do this in partnership with his followers. May God give us a holy fear of him and a renewed confidence that he will complete what he has started. The next chapter focuses on his followers, the body of Christ. It focuses on how they are to relate together as they represent the Godhead on earth and participate in God's mission.

6

Partnership and the Body of Christ

Introduction

The unfolding story of the Triune God continues as the purpose of God is manifested in the people of God. The One-in-Three has chosen to incorporate individuals into their community and this is reflected in the metaphors used to describe this expanding community. This chapter looks at the body of Christ, which is anchored in the Trinity. It examines similar metaphors and principles concerning the body. It inspects the standard of relationship that God requires for those in his family. It explores key biblical terms that inform partnership and specific examples of the body working together. These include several Pauline relationships, the Jerusalem offering, and the example of prayer. As with other sections, the study begins with the Trinity.

The Body of Christ and the Trinity

"There is one body and one Spirit – just as you were called to one hope when you were called – one Lord, one faith, one baptism; one God and Father of all, who is over all and through all and in all" (Eph 4:4–6). There are a few very significant passages in the New Testament that refer directly to the three Persons of the Trinity at the same time, and this is one. The context is that of the Apostle Paul pleading with the Ephesians to live right in relation to one another, as this is central to their identity in Christ. Paul refers to the high cost of following Christ as he confesses that he is a prisoner. He urges them to live a life worthy of their calling (Eph 4:1). He exhorts them to make every effort to live in unity. In this triadic passage the body is paired with the Spirit. It is the Spirit, as demonstrated in the previous chapter, which is the enabling power and presence in the lives of the believers. Their very existence is integrated with the Triune God. This permeation of the Holy Godhead into relationship with mankind is demonstrated throughout Paul's letters. Erickson explains:

> Arthur Wainwright has argued that in much of Paul's writing there is an implicit trinitarianism which shows itself even in the structure with which he organizes his letters. It is also present in the way he understands the church, for he describes it as the people of God, the body of Christ, and the temple of the Holy Spirit.[1]

The body of Christ is rooted in the Trinity. Bruce sees, within these few verses, the nature of an early Christian *credo*. The repetition of the numerical "one" points to the early Eastern creeds.[2] Before looking at the body metaphor, which is the most complete metaphor given in the New Testament, several similar images will be examined to add to the wealth of this imagery.

The Body of Christ: Metaphors

God has chosen several vivid images to explain his relationship with mankind. They focus on relationship and interconnectedness, both vertically with God and horizontally with man. He uses the metaphors of a building, branches, temple, and people of God.

Building

The community of God is not static; it is growing. The metaphor of the followers of God as a "building" focuses on this growth. The growth is only seen in connection with the rest of the building. It is a spiritual structure. It is a structure that is being expanded in a meticulous way.

> Consequently, you are no longer foreigners and aliens, but fellow citizens with God's people and members of God's household,

---

1. Millard J. Erickson, *Christian Theology, Vol 3* (Grand Rapids, MI: Baker, 1985), 1034–1035.

2. F. F. Bruce, *The Epistles to the Colossians, to Philemon, and to the Ephesians* (Grand Rapids, MI: Eerdmans, 1984), 335.

built on the foundation of the apostles and prophets, with Christ Jesus himself as the chief cornerstone. In him the whole building is joined together and rises to become a holy temple in the Lord. (Eph 2:19–21)

God the Son is the chief cornerstone of the foundation on which Christians have been firmly placed. The verb "built upon" (ἐποικοδομέω) is an aorist passive. The aorist stresses the completed action. Paul continues by saying the whole building is joined together. This verb, συναρμολογέομαι, has the meaning "to fit together in a coherent and compatible manner."[3] It is a present participle and, therefore, stresses the continuing action of the verb. Christians are being "continuously fitted together harmoniously in the process of building (present [2:21; 4:16]). The result is that the whole building is to be one perfect outcome of a continuous increase and growth (2:21; 4:12, 16)."[4] A main emphasis in this metaphor is the interconnectedness of the parts. They are joined and fitted together by God.

Branches

"I am the vine; you are the branches. If a man remains in me and I in him, he will bear much fruit; apart from me you can do nothing" (John 15:5). The metaphor here pictures a garden. God the Father is the gardener, and the one true vine is God the Son (John 15:1). A main focus of this picture is the concept of bearing fruit. The word "fruit" (καρπός) is used eight times in John 5:1–16. The emphasis is not the interconnectedness of the parts of the building, although this concept is present, but on the direct connection to the life source, which is the Lord Jesus Christ. Every branch must have a vital and living connection to the source; only then will there be the fruit that the branches were designed to produce. The desired fruit is described later on in John 15:16 as eternal fruit, fruit that will last. "You did not choose me, but I chose you and appointed you to go and bear fruit – fruit that will last. Then the Father will give you whatever you ask in my name." The fruit itself is completely interconnected to the purpose of God. God "chose" (ἐξελεξάμην – aorist middle indicative) his people, and he appointed them for fruit. This appointment is intertwined with the purpose and task of the Lord Jesus

---

3. Louw & Nida, *Greek-English Lexicon*.
4. Earl D. Radmacher, *What the Church Is All About: A Biblical and Historical Study* (Chicago, IL: Moody Press, 1972), 274.

Christ. "The verb rendered 'appointed' is ἔθηκα which is the verb used also of Christ's laying down of his life for his people (10:11, 15, 17f.; 15:13)."[5] The metaphor of the branches emphasizes the connection to the source and that each branch has been designed to bear abundant fruit according to God's eternal purpose.

Temple

The metaphor of "building," revealed in Ephesians 2, pointed to the construction of a "living" community. This community becomes "a holy temple in the Lord" (Eph 2:21). This image of the people of God as a temple is stated in 1 Corinthians 3:16–17: "Don't you know that you yourselves are God's temple and that God's Spirit lives in you? If anyone destroys God's temple, God will destroy him; for God's temple is sacred, and you are that temple." There is an individual and corporate identity in being part of the temple of God. Patterson explains that there were two main words for "temple" in the New Testament. One referred to the temple complex, and the other referred to the Holy of Holies. It is this second word, "temple of God" (ναὸς θεοῦ), which is used of the people of God. In this metaphor God's people are described as a holy group, indwelt by the living God.

Family

The metaphor of the family comes from the application within Scripture of familial names to those within the community of God. 2 Corinthians 6:18 says: "I will be a Father to you, and you will be my sons and daughters, says the Lord Almighty." Paul, in his letter to the Corinthians, refers to the Old Testament (2 Sam 7:14; Isa 43:6) as he draws on the picture of God's people as a family. He makes a distinction between those within the family of God and those outside. "Therefore, as we have opportunity, let us do good to all people, especially to those who belong to the family of believers" (Gal 6:10). Literally, the Greek word is "household of God" and is the dwelling that contains the family unit.

In his letter to Timothy, Paul uses family vocabulary in giving council on how to treat God's people. "Do not rebuke an older man harshly, but exhort him as if he were your father. Treat younger men as brothers, older women as

---

5. Leon Morris, *The Gospel according to John* (Grand Rapids, MI: Eerdmans, 1971), 676.

mothers, and younger women as sisters, with absolute purity" (1 Tim 5:1–2). While on earth, Christ linked obedience with identification with the Father as part of his family. "Pointing to his disciples, he said, 'Here are my mother and my brothers. For whoever does the will of my Father in heaven is my brother and sister and mother'"(Matt 12:49–50). The metaphor of "family" emphasizes the closeness of the individual relationships and the responsibility of bearing the family name by being obedient to the Father.

People of God

God, in his love, redeemed and reconciled mankind. Those who follow Christ are in a new category. They are those who have received the great heavenly gifts of forgiveness and mercy. "Once you were not a people, but now you are the people of God; once you had not received mercy, but now you have received mercy" (1 Pet 2:10). Paul writes, "What agreement is there between the temple of God and idols? For we are the temple of the living God. As God has said: 'I will live with them and walk among them, and I will be their God, and they will be my people'" (2 Cor 6:16).

Each of the different metaphors reveals a unique perspective of the "people of God" and their relationship to him and to one another. God's people are interconnected and joined together by him. Their strength comes from being connected to the source, and they are designed to bear fruit. They are a Holy group, indwelt by the Spirit. They are a family bearing together the name of the Father. This is a sobering thought for an individual, a local church, a mission agency, or a strategic partnership. In whatever form the people of God find themselves, they are not alone; they are part of something bigger by the design of God. The most extensive metaphor revealed in Scripture is that of the human body. The following section demonstrates how God's people fit together as they relate to others in God's purpose.

The Body of Christ: Principles

Paul spends much effort in explaining what the new reconciled community of God is like. The body has a purpose, an identity, and a way to function, all in line with the community of the Godhead who birthed it. Radmacher states:

> No metaphor can ever fully represent the entity to which it is applied. This is precisely why Paul uses several metaphors to describe the church. The metaphor of the body, however,

is the only one with which he actually equates the church (Eph 1:22–23). A comparison to the human body becomes for Paul the most descriptive and most accurate way to picture this corporate body of believers. When, therefore, the apostle Paul refers to the "church, which is his body" (Eph 1: 22-23), he is clearly likening one thing that has real ontological reality to another concrete reality, with a view to clarifying and pictorially describing the first.[6]

There are two passages that will be examined that highlight the body metaphor. The first is Romans 12:4–5, and the second is 1 Corinthians 12:12-27.

Unity and Diversity (Rom 12:4–5)

"Just as each of us has one body with many members, and these members do not all have the same function, so in Christ we who are many form one body, and each member belongs to all the others" (Rom 12:4-5). Within the metaphor of the body, there is a reflection of the unity and diversity revealed within the Godhead. God sees the body as one, singular, yet made up of distinct parts. F. F. Bruce points out that, "Diversity, not uniformity, is the mark of God's handiwork. It is so in nature; it is so in grace, too, and nowhere more so than in the Christian community. Here are many men and women with the most diverse kinds of parentage, environment, temperament, and capacity."[7] Diversity is not something to disparage but to embrace. It reflects the creative genius of Almighty God. God has determined that each part would have its own function. This word πρᾶξις is defined as a "sustained activity or responsibility."[8] It is an assignment given by God to the individual part for the sake of the greater whole. The oneness of the whole is demonstrated by the interrelationships of the parts. They belong to each other. This clear focus on relationship is central to the "body" metaphor. "The relationship of believers to each other is far more intimate than that between the members of any external organization, whether civil or ecclesiastical. It is analogous to the mutual relation of the members of the same body, animated by one soul."[9]

---

6. Radmacher, *What the Church*, 234–235.

7. F. F. Bruce, *The Epistle of Paul to the Romans: An Introduction and Commentary* (Grand Rapids, MI: Eerdmans, 1977), 226.

8. Louw and Nida, *Greek-English Lexicon*.

9. Charles Hodge, *Romans* (Wheaton, IL: Crossway, 1993), 347.

This interrelatedness of the parts of the body is demonstrated in more detail in the first letter to the Corinthians.

Parts of the Body (1 Cor 12:12–27)

> The body is a unit, though it is made up of many parts; and though all its parts are many, they form one body. So it is with Christ. For we were all baptized by one Spirit into one body – whether Jews or Greeks, slave or free – and we were all given the one Spirit to drink. Now the body is not made up of one part but of many. If the foot should say, "Because I am not a hand, I do not belong to the body," it would not for that reason cease to be part of the body. And if the ear should say, "Because I am not an eye, I do not belong to the body," it would not for that reason cease to be part of the body. If the whole body were an eye, where would the sense of hearing be? If the whole body were an ear, where would the sense of smell be? But in fact God has arranged the parts in the body, every one of them, just as he wanted them to be. If they were all one part, where would the body be? As it is, there are many parts, but one body. The eye cannot say to the hand, "I don't need you!" And the head cannot say to the feet, "I don't need you!" On the contrary, those parts of the body that seem to be weaker are indispensable, and the parts that we think are less honorable we treat with special honor. And the parts that are unpresentable are treated with special modesty, while our presentable parts need no special treatment. But God has combined the members of the body and has given greater honor to the parts that lacked it, so that there should be no division in the body, but that its parts should have equal concern for each other. If one part suffers, every part suffers with it; if one part is honored, every part rejoices with it. Now you are the body of Christ, and each one of you is a part of it. (1 Cor 12:12–27)

Paul gives tremendous insight into the inner workings of the community of God. In this particular passage, he emphasizes unity and diversity. He makes it clear that God is the source of the diversity and addresses the human tendency of wanting to elevate a certain part over another.

Diversity of the Parts

The Corinthian church was diverse. The city of Corinth was known for its wickedness and debauchery. It was a cosmopolitan melting pot populated by Greeks, Asians, and Italians. "The constituency of the Corinthian congregation reflected the city itself and in what was largely a classless church with a wide racial mixture, including people of varied moral and spiritual histories."[10] Diversity of race and of social class does not prevent incorporation into one body. Culturally, Jews remain Jews and Greeks remain Greeks. A person's economic situation does not change; the rich are still rich and the poor are still poor. There were real differences in the composition of the Corinthian church. These differences did not go away. However, there is another spiritual reality at work: "the various national and social groups, and the dissident religious cliques at Corinth (i.II f.), have all entered into the unity of the body of Christ, which they ought to express, and not deny, by means of their various gifts."[11] Jesus Christ is Lord of all peoples. His church reflects that diversity.

Each Part Belongs

The church in Corinth had numerous problems. Paul addresses the issue of diversity and unity in an attempt to bring honor to each and every part of the body of Christ. The diversity led to jealousy and confusion concerning spiritual gifts and what it meant to be part of the body. Paul gives two examples in verses 15–16, each making the argument that a person is deceived if they think they are not a part of the body because they do not have a specific role or gift. The significance of each part is found in Christ, not in their function. Every part belongs and is important to the body of Christ.

God Arranged the Parts

"But in fact God has arranged the parts in the body, every one of them, just as he wanted them to be." The verb for God arranged is ἔθετο. This is the same word examined in John 15:16 concerning believers being appointed to bear fruit. God has appointed and arranged each individual part. God himself has done it. It is born out of his sovereign will for his sovereign purpose. He did it according to his desire or will, θέλω. With this proclamation comes the understanding that if God did it, then it is good, and it is acceptable. No

---

10. Paige Patterson, *The Troubled Triumphant Church* (Nashville, TN: Thomas Nelson, 1983), 14.

11. C. K. Barrett, *Harper's New Testament Commentaries: A Commentary on the First Epistle to the Corinthians* (New York: Harper & Row, 1968), 289.

person can take issue with this determination, or if they do, they need to take issue with God himself as to why he got it wrong. No one can belittle any of God's appointments. No one can come up with a better plan or a better mix of parts for the good of the whole.

Each Part Is Indispensable
Man tends to put value on roles and outward appearances. In opposition to this is God's determination that, in his eyes, all the parts are necessary and are eternally equal. What some would call weaker parts, God calls indispensable. The word ἀναγκαῖος is defined as "pertaining to being necessary and indispensable to the occurrence of some event – 'necessary, indispensable.'"[12] Within the community God has created, there are different roles. Each role is valued and necessary, no matter how large or small. God combined each part.

God Combined the Parts
It is stressed again in verse 24 that God is in total control of the design and composition of his body. He "combined" the parts. The word is συνεκέρασεν. It is defined as "to cause parts to fit together in an overall arrangement – 'to put together, to compose, to structure.'"[13] There is an acknowledgement that different parts have a more presentable role than others. This does not affect their honor or importance within the body. Each part is combined exactly the way God desires.

Equality amongst the Parts
There is just one body. There is one God, one Lord, and one Spirit. All believers belong to the one body. Therefore, there should be no divisions. The root of the word "division" means "to split, to tear." It takes on the meaning of division or discord or division into opposing groups.[14] Division starts when different parts are not honored and God not recognized as the author of the parts. Man tries to impose his own order on the body and raise his own part to a more honored position. When there is honor and equal concern for the different parts, God's body functions as it should. This "equal" concern has an emotional aspect: μεριμνάω (derivative of μέριμνα – "worry") "to have an anxious concern, based on apprehension about possible danger

---

12. Louw & Nida, *Greek-English Lexicon*.
13. Ibid.
14. Ibid.

or misfortune" – "to be worried about, to be anxious about."[15] It reflects a genuine interest and concern for the other parts that make up the body. There is a recognition that God is in control and that he has created and ordained each person for his role. To love and honor God is to love and honor his people as he made them. The above principles of the body are key elements in any healthy partnership. When God's people follow God's directions, fruit is the result. If these principles are lacking, there is every kind of disorder, competition, and strife. Those who follow God recognize that there is only one head to each body. To this spiritual body, that head is no other than the Lord Jesus Christ.

Christ Is the Head

When it comes to considering the picture of the human body, it is clear that the most important part is the head. As it relates to the family of God, the picture of God's people as the body of Christ reveals the overall supremacy of the Lord Jesus Christ. Jesus has many titles in his role as part of the Godhead. He is revealed as the head of the church. Paul goes into detail on the headship of Christ, particularly in the letters to the Ephesians and the Colossians.

The awesome power and authority of God is demonstrated through the death and resurrection of Christ Jesus. Satan has been defeated, evil conquered, and the shame of the cross has turned into unimaginable glory. The Son of God has been lifted up and seated at the right hand of the Father. His reigning state is described in finite letters and words that do not even begin to reflect his position and power. Paul writes:

> That power is like the working of his mighty strength, which he exerted in Christ when he raised him from the dead and seated him at his right hand in the heavenly realms, far above all rule and authority, power and dominion, and every title that can be given, not only in the present age but also in the one to come. (Eph 1:19–21)

It is this Jesus, this conqueror, under whose feet God has placed everything; he is all-powerful. Paul reveals, in addition, that God himself has appointed Jesus to be head over everything for the church. The church is described here in Ephesians 1:23 is an extension of Christ. The church is the

---

15. Ibid.

fullness of him who fills everything in every way. Paul repeats this truth later in the letter, in Ephesians 5:23. He states that Christ is the head of the church. The church is his body, and he is its Savior.

In the book of Colossians, Paul explains the headship of Christ again to a different group of believers. "And he is the head of the body, the church; he is the beginning and the firstborn from among the dead, so that in everything he might have the supremacy" (Col 1:18). Every power and authority is under him. In Colossians 2:19 Paul brings to their attention the plight of people who have lost their way and focused on their own insights. Such a person is no longer connected to the head. The head is Christ. The whole body is revealed as growing from the head. God himself causes it to grow, yet only through this connection with the head. William Barclay paints this picture of the head-body relationship:

> The church is the body of Christ, that is, the organism through which He acts and which He shares all His experiences. But, humanly speaking, the body is the servant of the head and is powerless without it. So Jesus Christ is the guiding spirit of the Church: it is at His bidding that the Church must live and move. Without him the Church cannot think the truth, cannot act correctly, cannot decide its direction.[16]

In the context of partnership, there is a clear recognition that Jesus is supreme. Every effort, action, strategy, and relationship falls under his Lordship. Christ is the ultimate authority, and all who call on his name must live and act in subject to his authority. This includes what they do in association with the purpose of God and how they do it as they relate to others who are also in submission to Christ and are part of the same family. The next section examines the expectations of Christ for his people as they work and live together.

The Body of Christ: Interpersonal Relationships

Walter Wright, in his commentary on Ephesians, explains who makes up the membership of the church: "The church then is constituted of those who, in this present age, have seen the son and have believed on him, having been drawn by the Father, with the promise and prospect of eternal life – of sinners

---

16. William Barclay, *The Letters to the Philippians, Colossians, and Thessalonians* (Philadelphia, PA: Westminster Press, 1975), 120–121.

who have been called to be Saints."[17] As one enters into this new family, there is a host of expectations and a way to live and treat others that flow from the very Godhead itself. No longer are people members of the world, but they are members of a "royal" family. They need to behave in a way that reflects their family heritage, which has Christ as the Supreme Head and the supreme example of how to live and relate to others. Paul, writing to the churches in Galatia, commands them to live by the Spirit. The immediate context is telling. "If you keep on biting and devouring each other, watch out or you will be destroyed by each other. So I say, live by the Spirit, and you will not gratify the desires of the sinful nature" (Gal 5:15–16). He continues in verse 25, "Since we live by the Spirit, let us keep in step with the Spirit. Let us not become conceited, provoking and envying each other." To be part of the family and in obedience to the head means to be following the Spirit. Behavior is key to being part of God's family. Paul tells the saints in Ephesus:

> As a prisoner for the Lord, then, I urge you to live a life worthy of the calling you have received. Be completely humble and gentle; be patient, bearing with one another in love. Make every effort to keep the unity of the Spirit through the bond of peace. There is one body and one Spirit – just as you were called to one hope, when you were called one Lord, one faith, one baptism; one God and Father of all, who is over all and through all and in all. (Eph 4:1–6)

Paul points to the oneness of the faith. Each individual that enters into the family of God enters into the oneness that is represented in the Holy Godhead. In these potent verses Paul references one Spirit, one Lord and one God and Father of all. The life of a believer is totally intertwined with the Godhead. Barclay comments, "It is the Christian belief that we live in a God-created, God-controlled, God-sustained, God-filled world."[18] Therefore, there is no place for disunity amongst God's people. Paul makes the plea for the saints to make every effort for unity. Relationship is central to the three persons of the Godhead, and it is central to the Family that they have begotten.

To the saints in Christ Jesus at Philippi Paul repeats the same theme:

---

17. Walter C. Wright, *Ephesians* (Chicago, IL: Moody Press, 1954), 64.
18. William Barclay, *The Letters to the Galatians and Ephesians* (Philadelphia, PA: Westminster Press, 1975), 143.

> If you have any encouragement from being united with Christ, if any comfort from his love, if any fellowship with the Spirit, if any tenderness and compassion, then make my joy complete by being like minded, having the same love, being one in spirit and purpose. (Phil 2:1–2)

The unity that Paul expounds includes an outward manifestation that is a result of them being of one mind and purpose. That oneness comes from individuals plugging into the one source. That source is Christ. It is his life and his purposes that are the standard to which every one of his followers must strive. Finally, in writing to the holy and faithful brothers in Colosse, he states:

> Therefore as God's chosen people, holy and dearly loved, clothe yourselves with compassion, kindness, humility, gentleness and patience. Bear with each other and forgive whatever grievances you may have against one another. Forgive as the Lord forgave you. And over all these virtues put on love, which binds them all together in perfect unity. (Col 3:12–14)

Right relationships amongst God's people are based in the Trinity. Individuals enter into God's family, where there is only one faith, one body, one Spirit, one Lord, and one God and Father of all. The Trinity is defined by oneness. The body of Christ is also defined by oneness. There is no room for any other view or behavior. As God's people live and minister together, they must understand that God himself has made people different. Believers are different in terms of the ministries they have been assigned and the role or part they have in the greater body of Christ, as given and determined by God. The next section explores positive examples of God's people working together as part of the body of Christ.

The Body of Christ: Working Together

Throughout Paul's journeys he met hundreds of people, and his letters are full of special relationships that he established along the way. These relationships were centered on Christ and ministry together for the sake of the gospel. They are varied and rich in the type of people and in the locations in which they took place. These relationships again demonstrate the oneness of the body of Christ but also, more importantly, their unity and collaboration in accomplishing God's purpose. All those in the family of God and working for the kingdom of God are connected by the head and bonded together in their service. Several Greek terms are prominent as Paul describes his partnership with other individuals, and they will be considered next.

The Body in Action: Biblical Terms

Paul uses several key terms to demonstrate the interconnectedness that they have as part of God's family and as workers in accomplishing God's missionary task. These terms are "fellow workers," "partnership," and "fellow soldier."

Fellow Worker (συνεργός)

The first word, *sunergos,* is a compound word made up of the preposition *sun,* which denotes "union, with or together." The second part, *ergon,* means "work, employment or task." Collin Brown translates the word as "colleague, a fellow-worker, an assistant."[19] Baur, Arndt, and Gingrich, in examining the use of this word, states, "Paul refers to those who helped him in spreading the gospel as his fellow workers."[20] This term is used of Priscilla and Aquila, Urbanus, and Timothy in Paul's personal greetings at the end of his letter to the Saints in Rome. In the Philippian letter Paul lists a group of associates, "Yes, and I ask you, loyal yokefellow, help these women who have contended at my side in the cause of the gospel, along with Clement and the rest of my fellow workers whose names are in the book of life" (Phil 4:3). In a unique way, the term is used not of being fellow workers with Paul but of being a fellow worker with God. This term is used of Timothy in 1 Thessalonians 3:2 and of Paul and Apollos in their service towards the Corinthians. In further describing the word *sunergos,* Colin Brown states:

> It reports that the Lord worked with the disciples confirming their word by the accompanying signs. It is true that this accompanying work of God is the decisive element in all missionary activity; but it is a real co-working, in as much as the person who has been called by God to be a witness is himself no mere inactive instrument in the proclaiming event, but equally a

---

19. Brown, *New International Dictionary Vol. III* (Grand Rapids, MI: Zondervan, 1971), 1147.

20. Walter Baur, *A Greek-English Lexicon of the New Testament and Other Early Christian Literature,* trans. William F. Arndt and F. Wilbur Gingrich (Chicago, IL: University of Chicago Press, 1957), 795.

cooperating servant of God. Paul can therefore formulate it thus: *theou gar esmen synergoi*, "we are God's fellow-workers."[21]

The word reveals collaboration. It unveils the joining together of God's people in the task of God's purpose. Those who make up the community of faith are joined together in a spiritual family with a spiritual task. This community or fellowship is represented by the special word *koinonia*, which is looked at next.

Partnership (κοινωνία)

There is a special connection between those called of God to do the work of God. Paul uses the word *koinonia* to represent that special partnership. According to Vines, the noun *koinonos* means "Partake, Partaker." "*Koinonos*, an adjective, signifying having in common (*koinos, common*), is used as a noun, denoting a companion, partner, partaker."[22] This particular word is used only twice in this form in the Epistles of Paul. It is used of Philemon and of Epaphraditus, both considered as partners with Paul. The word group also contains the word *koinonia*, which is translated as "fellowship." Vine defines the word as "communion, fellowship, sharing in common."[23] Baur defines the usage as: association, communion, fellowship and close relationship. It is used in this sense of fellowship with the Son (1 Cor 1:9), fellowship with the Holy Spirit (Phil 2:1), and as having a close relationship with the gospel (Phil 1:5). In this last verse, it is Paul addressing all the saints in Philippi as those who are partnering with him in the gospel. In examining the concept of *koinonia*, Alvarez quotes Brinkman: "*Koinonia* means that the visible bond with God that, at the same time, is the bond of the new community, is the sign and the instrument of God's reconciling purpose."[24] It is clear that there is a special bond and community amongst those who make up the family of God. This bond is not only represented in the relationship as brothers and sisters, but also in the task that they are commissioned to be a part of, which is the Great Commission. This is demonstrated by the use of the term "fellow soldiers."

---

21. Brown, *New International Dictionary*, 1152.
22. W. E. Vine, *An Expository Dictionary of New Testament Words* (Old Tappan, NJ: Fleming H. Revell, 1966), 161.
23. Ibid., 90.
24. Alvarez, "Sharing in God's Mission," 19.

Fellow Soldier (συστρατιώτης)

Sustratiotes: This is a compound word made up of the preposition *"sun"* which denotes "union," "with" or "together" along with the common word for "soldier," *stratiotes*. Therefore, the term is used as "fellow soldier." Bauer describes the limited usage as follows: "... in our literature only figuratively of those who devote themselves to service of the gospel."[25] Louw and Nida describe it as "one who serves in arduous tasks or undergoes severe experiences together with someone else – one who struggles along with, one who works arduously along with, fellow struggler." This term was applied to several of Paul's co-workers. Having looked at the definition of these terms, it is good to see them used in real-life settings.

The Body in Action: Individual Relationships

These three key partnership terms are further explored by examining them in the context of the individuals with whom Paul worked as he participated in God's mission. The first individual to be looked at is Epaphroditus.

Epaphroditus

Paul spoke very highly about Epaphroditus. They had shared in real-life events together for the sake of Christ. Concerning this brother, D. Edmond Hiebert writes:

> Paul spoke in glowing terms of Epaphroditus, whom he was sending back to Philippi. He declared his own close relations to him by calling him "my brother and fellow-worker and fellow-soldier" (2:25). His "my" goes with all three terms which are united under one article in the original. Arranged in an ascending scale, the three picture an ideal Christian relationship. "Brother" unites them in a fellowship of faith, for they are brothers in the Lord; "fellow-worker" unites them in a partnership of toil, working in the furtherance of the gospel; and "fellow-soldier" unites them as comrades in arms, jointly engaged in combat with the forces of evil. With this honorable testimony to him, Paul set forth the essence of the high ministry for which Epaphroditus

---

25. Baur, *Greek-English Lexicon*, 803.

enlisted in coming to Rome. Paul said nothing finer of any of his other companions in toil.[26]

Here is a tremendous example of family life. There was such a strong bond between Paul and the believers in Philippi that the church sent Epaphroditus to help meet his needs while he was imprisoned in Rome. Paul tells us that he almost died in fulfilling this service (Phil 2:30). This is a beautiful demonstration of love: that which Epaphroditus had for Paul and the love the church had for Paul. The believers in Philippi also had a huge love for their own member as they heard of his close call with death as he risked his life for the work of Christ. The next person to be examined is Titus.

Titus

In 2 Corinthians 8:23, Paul explains to the believers in Corinth that he is sending a delegation made up of honorable saints to them for the purpose of collecting an offering to be sent to those suffering in Jerusalem. It is Paul's description of Titus that is revealing. He describes him as his "partner" and his "fellow worker." The word "partner" is *koinonos,* and the term "fellow worker" is *sunergos.* D. Edmond Hiebert reveals insightful qualities as he examines the life of Titus:

> From the difficult tasks that Paul assigned to him, it is clear that Paul considered Titus a capable and trustworthy co-laborer, possessing a forceful personality. He was capable, energetic, tactful, resourceful, skillful in handling men and affairs, and effective in conciliating people. Naturally more aggressive than Timothy, he could not only take orders but also take the initiative in the face of challenging circumstances. He breathed the spirit of Paul, and in his conduct, manifested the same unmercenary attitude that characterized Paul.[27]

Paul's picture here is one of joint service in a specific task, that of the collecting an offering for the brethren in Jerusalem. It is not a life-or-death task but one that expresses the concept of partnership. The next person to be considered is Philemon.

---

26. D. Edmond Hiebert, *Personalities around Paul* (Chicago, IL: Moody Press, 1973), 158.
27. Ibid., 114.

Philemon

In this short personal letter from Paul, we see a multitude of relationships as Paul addresses individuals and also the "assembly" (*ekklesia*) that meets in their home. It is a house fellowship, and Paul uses special terms as he addresses individuals. He calls Philemon a "fellow worker" (*sunergo*). Later, in verse 17, Paul refers to their "partnership" (*koinonia*). N. T. Wright comments:

> The idea we need to grasp – the theme that dominates the letter – is that, in Christ, Christians not only belong to one another but actually become mutually identified, truly rejoicing with the happy and genuinely weeping with the sad (Rom 12:15; cf. 1 Cor 12:26; 2 Cor 11:28–29). *Koinonia* is part of the truth about the body of Christ. All are bound together in a mutual bond that makes our much-prized individualism look shallow and petty.[28]

Paul acknowledges not just the partnership with Philemon but also with the local church. The last person to reflect upon is Phoebe.

Phoebe

In Paul's salutations at the end of his letter to all the saints in Rome, he highlights several dozen individuals and assemblies, but he begins the list with a special note concerning a dear sister named Phoebe (Rom 16:1). She is described as a servant in the church in Cenchrae, and she is going to be making a trip to Rome. Paul demonstrates, in a practical way, the interrelationship between believers in separate cities. He is networking his relationships and calling on his brethren in Rome to respond in a manner worthy of being a member in the body of Christ. D. E. Hiebert explains:

> Paul further requested that they "assist" or stand by her to aid her, "in whatsoever business she hath need of you" (KJV). Such assistance would require their time and effort, yet he was confident that as Christians they would readily do this for this worthy Christian Woman. Stifler comments, "What a charitable free masonry existed in the church! Her 'business' was her own, but Paul does not hesitate to call on the whole Roman brotherhood to stand by her in it."[29]

---

28. N. T. Wright, *Colossians and Philemon*, Tyndale New Testament Commentaries (Grand Rapids, MI: Eerdmans, 1986), 176.

29. Hiebert, *Personalities around Paul*, 200.

There are key terms used by Paul in his letters that disclose the deep relationships and collaboration happening within the body of Christ. Whether between individuals, between fellowships, or whichever combination, these words stand out. Individuals and churches are "partners" in the gospel. They are "fellow workers" with Paul. They are "fellow soldiers." They are God's people, listening to God's Spirit, working for God's purposes, boldly representing the gospel of Christ to the world. They come from many different geographic and cultural backgrounds. One of the greatest examples of this type of partnership in the New Testament is the mobilization of the Gentile church to help the impoverished Jewish believers in Jerusalem.

The Body in Action: The Jerusalem Offering

The examples of partnership presented so far have mostly been Paul's relationship to other people as they worked together for God's glory. There are a few places in Scripture where there are multiple groups coming together to accomplish a specific purpose, such as the taking of the land in Joshua's day and the rebuilding of the wall in Nehemiah's day. In the New Testament the most prominent is the Jerusalem offering, which is referred to in depth in 2 Corinthians, chapters 8 and 9. Three other passages are related to this offering: Romans 15:25-32, 1 Corinthians 16:1-4, and Galatians 2:9-10. The church in Jerusalem was facing a terrible time. It was weakened by persecution, it found itself in the midst of a famine, and the church was poverty stricken.[30] Even though Paul was called as the apostle to the Gentiles, his heart was always with his Jewish people. A result of the Jerusalem Council was a challenge from the leadership in Jerusalem for Paul to not forget the poor as he carried out his mission to the gentiles. This is revealed in Paul's letter to the Galatians, "James, Peter and John, those reputed to be pillars, gave me and Barnabas the right hand of fellowship when they recognized the grace given to me. They agreed that we should go to the Gentiles, and they to the Jews. All they asked was that we should continue to remember the poor, the very thing I was eager to do" (Gal 2:9-10). Paul had not forgot the church in Jerusalem, and their financial situation weighed heavily on his heart. Paul understood the connection between the Gentile church and the Messianic church as being one in Christ. Tom Wright shares that Paul, in writing to the Corinthians

---

30. J. Vernon McGee, *II Corinthians* (La Verne, CA: El Camino Press, 1977), 95.

> . . . wants them to share in the great project he has in hand: demonstrating to the Gentile churches that they are part of the same family as the Jewish Christians in Jerusalem, and, still more important, demonstrating to the Jewish Christians that those strange, uncircumcised Gentiles who, like them, have come to believe in Jesus the Messiah are fellow members with them in God's renewed people, the family defined by their faith in the risen Jesus as Lord.[31]

In order to address the issue in Jerusalem, Paul created a partnership amongst the Gentile churches. Their task was to collect an offering and safely deliver it to their brothers and sisters in need in Jerusalem. Paul mentions the churches in Macedonia (2 Cor 8:1), which would include the cities of Philippi and Thessalonica, as well as the region of Achaia where Corinth was situated, as being involved in this partnership. This was a multi-cultural multi-local church collaboration. The impetus for the offering was bound up in the purpose of God. The word "grace" is used by Paul ten times in Second Corinthians chapters 8 and 9. He uses this word grace, "to refer to what God wants to do not just *in* and *for* Christians but *through* them."[32] This act of obedience by the churches was to impact them as well as those in Jerusalem (2 Cor 9:12–15). It is also important to note that this was not a one-directional flow of blessing. Yes, in terms of funds, the Jerusalem church was in need, and the Gentile churches were responding; however, Paul makes it clear that the Gentile churches have been on the receiving end, as well:

> For Macedonia and Achaia were pleased to make a contribution for the poor among the saints in Jerusalem. They were pleased to do it, and indeed they owe it to them. For if the Gentiles have shared in the Jews' spiritual blessings, they owe it to the Jews to share with them their material blessings. (Rom 15: 26–27)

Diversity was demonstrated in that churches were asked to give what they could; there was not a pre-determined set amount. The collaboration was strengthened through the appointment of the churches of representatives who would join Paul in the delivery of the gift (2 Cor 8:19, 23). It was a high priority for Paul that the management of the funds would be done in

---

31. Tom Wright, *Paul for Everyone: 2 Corinthians* (Louisville, KY: Westminster John Knox Press, 2004), 84.

32. Ibid., 86.

a transparent and Godly way. He cared that it was done right and that all could attest that it was done right (2 Cor 8:20–21). Paul knew that there was a spiritual battle connected with this service. He wanted all involved to be blessed and to be a blessing. Even for the saints in Jerusalem to receive an offering from Gentiles, he knew there were spiritual issues. Because of this, he enlisted the saints in Rome to pray for him and the offering. He states:

> Now, however, I am on my way to Jerusalem in the service of the saints there. For Macedonia and Achaia were pleased to make a contribution for the poor among the saints in Jerusalem. They were pleased to do it, and indeed they owe it to them. For if the Gentiles have shared in the Jews' spiritual blessings, they owe it to the Jews to share with them their material blessings . . . Pray that I may be rescued from the unbelievers in Judea and that my service in Jerusalem may be acceptable to the saints there. (Rom 15:25–27, 31)

The Jerusalem offering is an excellent example of God's people from multiple backgrounds working together in obedience to God. This particular partnership included a regional group of churches and a missionary band. In the world today, because of gains in communication, multitudes of believers can play the part that the church in Rome played by joining with God and other believers through prayer in accomplishing God's purposes. The powerful collaboration with God in prayer is explored further in the next section.

The Body in Action: Prayer

The oneness of God's people has been demonstrated above in terms of their relationship together and their participation in the mission of God. Central to all of this while on earth is the very practical outworking of the action of intercession. Arthur Glasser writes of Paul and the strategic aspect of prayer:

> Paul prayed for both the present extension of the Kingdom among the unconverted and for its eschatological consummation, as Jesus had instructed. While he was truly concerned for the Kingdom and its final manifestation in glory, he was equally

burdened for the physical, social, and spiritual needs of the people of his own generation.[33]

Intercession is a vital ministry of the body of Christ. It is the one item that links individuals, assemblies of believers, the Holy Spirit, and the mission of God all into one. Paul constantly challenged people to pray, and it is worth the effort to examine what he asked them to do and why. It may be the purest and broadest form of collaboration that we see revealed in the Pauline Epistles.

Paul was concerned for the lost and knew that prayer was a key element in the process of the gospel going out. In his closing remarks to the Thessalonians, he requests, "Finally brothers, pray for us that the message of the Lord may spread rapidly and be honored, just as it was with you" (2 Thess 3:1). This is also demonstrated in Paul's letter to Timothy, "I urge, then, first of all, that requests, prayers, intercession and thanksgiving be made for everyone – for kings and all those in authority, that we may live peaceful and quiet lives in all godliness and holiness. This is good, and pleases God our savior, who wants all men to be saved and to come to a knowledge of the truth" (1 Tim 2:1–3).

Along with the application of intercession for the salvation of the lost, Paul also spent hours in intercession for individuals that he knew. He was very specific in his prayers and desired a deep spiritual growth in those he prayed for.

> Night and day we pray most earnestly that we may see you again and supply what is lacking in your faith. Now may our God and Father himself and our Lord Jesus clear the way for us to come to you. May the Lord make your love increase and overflow for each other and for everyone else, just as ours does for you. May he strengthen your hearts so that you will be blameless and holy in the presence of our God and Father when our Lord Jesus comes with all his holy ones. (1 Thess 3:10–13)

There was an interaction between Paul and his team and those that they met throughout their missionary journeys. They were connected through prayer as they interceded according to specific needs that they shared back and forth.

Paul also encourages those he has never met to join him in prayer. Paul pleads with those in Rome, "I urge you brothers, by our Lord Jesus Christ and by the love of the Spirit, to join me in my struggle by praying to God for me.

---

33. Glasser, *Announcing the Kingdom*, 294.

Pray that I may be rescued from the unbelievers in Judea and that my service in Jerusalem may be acceptable to the saints there" (Rom 15:30–31). Here is another example of the fullness of the Godhead being revealed, this time in the area of intercession. There is interconnectedness between Paul's struggles, the saints he is calling to join him by praying for him, and the Godhead who is involved at every level. Here we see a picture of the working of the family of God: different people in different places, yet one purpose through the unity of the body, all under the covering of the Triune God. As noted above, Paul, who constantly prayed for the Saints in Rome (Rom 1:9) and boldly asks them to pray for him (Rom 15:30), had never visited Rome and had not personally met the majority of the Saints there.

This interconnectedness in prayer is demonstrated again in Paul's letter to those in Corinth. "He has delivered us from such a deadly peril, and he will deliver us. On him we have set our hope that he will continue to deliver us, as you help us by your prayers. Then many will give thanks on our behalf for the gracious favor granted us in answer to the prayers of many" (2 Cor 1:10–11). This triangle of interconnectedness in prayer is seen in the example of an individual marked by Paul as a prayer warrior. This triangle between God, an individual, and a local fellowship is found in the letter to the Colossians, "Epaphras, who is one of you, and a servant of Christ Jesus, sends greetings. He is always wrestling in prayer for you, that you may stand firm in all the will of God, mature and fully assured" (Col 4:12). There is collaboration demonstrated here, and the ultimate source of the idea of interceding for others is from the Holy Spirit.

The depth of the involvement of the Spirit of God in the whole realm of intercession is revealed in Roman 8:26–27: "In the same way, the Spirit helps us in our weakness. We do not know what we ought to pray for, but the Spirit himself intercedes for us with groans that words cannot express. And he who searches our hearts knows the mind of the Spirit, because the Spirit intercedes for the saints in accordance with God's will." William Barclay believes this:

> The first two verses form one of the most important passages on prayer in the whole New Testament. Paul is saying that, because of our weakness, we do not know what to pray for, but the prayers we offer are offered for us by the Holy Spirit. C. H. Dodd defines

prayer in this way – "prayer is the divine in us appealing to the Divine above us."[34]

Prayer is revealed as a major discipline within the body of Christ. Paul continually encourages the saints to intercede. The focus of these prayers is on the lost in general and, more specifically, for other saints and their particular situations. It may be for their growth spiritually or for a circumstance in which they find themselves. At the heart of intercession is the Triune God. It is God's people joining in interceding for God's purposes to be accomplished. It is intertwined with the working and direction of the Holy Spirit. Intercession is the greatest example of the collaboration of the body of Christ, representing both the vertical relationship between man and God and man's horizontal relationship with other men.

Summary and Reflection

This study began by examining the Holy Trinity and then the purpose of God. Throughout the process, the working of the Godhead and the centrality of relationships have been revealed. God has a mission, and that is to see his gospel go out and people come into a believing relationship with him. This plan will come to fulfillment when the Lord comes back again. As people come from darkness to light through faith in Christ Jesus, they enter into a new paradigm. They become the people of God through the Holy Spirit. As part of the body of Christ, they recognize that Jesus is the head. There is no other. He is Lord and Savior, and his ways become the ways of his people. Individuals become part of the body of Christ and the family of God. These metaphors, along with others presented, represent the new relationships, both vertically and horizontally: vertically with the Godhead, and horizontally with fellow believers. Because believers are part of the family of God and are, therefore, part of God's purposes, their treatment of one another becomes paramount. They are to be in unity, having the same mind and purpose of Christ. Within this unity of the oneness of the body of Christ, there comes also the diversity of the family of God. God himself declares that his family is made up of unique individuals and that he himself has made them that way. There is unity and yet diversity. The diversity allows for the multiple parts of his body to be manifested for his glory and for the building up of his church.

---

34. William Barclay, *The Letter to the Romans* (Philadelphia, PA: Westminster Press, 1975), 110.

All of this is in line with the fulfillment of his sovereign plan. The example of the body of Christ working together for the fulfillment of God's purposes is seen clearly through the relationships displayed in the Pauline epistles – the relationship of Paul with local churches and individuals, and vice versa. It is also powerfully demonstrated through the ministry of intercession, where the people of God join together with the Spirit of God to intercede for one another and for those who have yet to come to faith in the Lord Jesus. The body of Christ sets the foundations for Christian partnership in missions. It proclaims that everyone is on the same team and that God has determined individual's roles. Jesus is the head, and the Holy Spirit is in control. Right relationship with God and with fellow believers is the expected standard of operation.

In reflection, the clear teaching of the Scriptures that God himself appoints roles and giftings is both a sobering and a humbling thought. It is sobering because it makes me stop and think, "Who is behind this person's ministry and calling?" Is it really Almighty God? Has God truly raised them up to do the ministry? Has he called them to do it in that way? Am I giving them the respect and the honor that their appointed role deserves? It is humbling because it also states that I, and those around me, have limits. I am called and designed to do a specific thing. There are things that I cannot do and should not do. My Western upbringing pushes me to think that I can do everything, or should at least attempt everything. In God's design, there are times when he says, "No, not you! There is someone else that I want to use. They will do it better than you in the power of my Holy Spirit. You need to stay within the roles and giftings that I have appointed for you." May God give us the grace to recognize in humility our roles and enable us through his Spirit to honor, respect, encourage, and bless others as they fulfill their roles.

Connected closely with the concept of the parts of the body that has been presented in chapter 6 are the gifts of the Holy Spirit. The gifts are the way that God empowers his people to accomplish his purposes. The next chapter examines the creative way that God has accomplished this by enhancing the need of his people to rely on one another to carry out his will.

7

Partnership and the Gifts of the Spirit

Introduction

Linked closely with the diversity of parts in the body of Christ is the concept of spiritual gifts. These gifts are prominent in the New Testament writings and a distinguishing mark of the church age. Christ told his disciples to wait for the Spirit (Acts 1:4). When the Spirit came, it would be the enabling power for their ministry and witness (Acts 1:8). This chapter examines spiritual gifts beginning with their source in the Trinity, their description, their purpose in the context of *missio Dei*, and their contribution to the understanding of partnership in Christian mission.

The Gifts: Based in the Trinity

This study began with a look at the Triune God. The involvement of the Trinity has been traced through the purpose of God and the body of Christ. The inter-connectedness of the Godhead in the distribution of spiritual gifts is revealed in this chapter. As with the purpose of God and the body of Christ, the Trinity is central. The emphasis on relationship remains core to the understanding of God and his dealing with man. One of the main triadic passages is found in the context of spiritual gifts. "There are different kinds of gifts, but the same Spirit. There are different kinds of service, but the same Lord. There are different kinds of working, but the same God works all of them in all men" (1 Cor 12:4–6). The word "different" is διαιρέσεις and means "to divide and distribute to persons on the basis of certain implied distinctions or differences . . . it is also possible to interpret διαίρεσις as meaning "difference" or "variety."[1] The first definition seems to be best. Barrett claims, "There are distributions (διαίρεσις not varieties, though this is implied; Paul thinks of the gifts as given, not in the abstract) *of gifts* (χάρισματα; see i. 7)."[2] In this same flow, Orr and Walther state, "The gifts are divine apportionments, and the uniqueness of their identity is to be found in the Spirit who gives them."[3] This word διαιρέσεις is used with all three persons of the Godhead. A unique corresponding noun is linked to each, which demonstrates the involvement of the Godhead. The Spirit is linked with "gifts" (χαρισμά), the Lord Jesus with "service" (διακονία) and God the Father with "works" (ἐνέργημα). The gifts originate with the Trinity and are distributed through the Holy Spirit. The oversight belongs to God, according to the purpose of God. Bridge and Phypers summarize it well:

> Particularly impressive is the way each Person of the Godhead is associated with different aspects of the gifts. Thus, since it is the special activity of the Holy Spirit to distribute, Paul speaks of His "gifts." As Jesus came not to be served but to serve, Paul speaks of His "varieties of service." Because God the Father is the source of all power, so Paul speaks of His "working." What tremendous activity, therefore is encompassed in the exercise of spiritual gifts! When a member of the body of Christ uses his gifts, the whole Trinity is at work in that one individual for the well being and blessing of others![4]

Paul continues in 1 Corinthians 12 to emphasize the role of the Holy Spirit as the distributor of the gifts. He makes a clear statement as to the origin and oversight of these gifts. "All these are the work of one and the same Spirit, and he gives them to each one, just as he determines" (1 Cor 12:11). The word "determine" (βούλομαι) means "to desire to have or experience something, with the implication of some reasoned planning or will to accomplish the goal."[5]

---

1. Louw & Nida, *Greek-English Lexicon*.
2. Barrett, *Harper's New Testament*, 283.
3. William F. Orr and James Arthur Walther, *First Corinthians* (New York: Doubleday, 1976), 281.
4. Donald Bridge and David Phypers, *Spiritual Gifts and the Church* (Downers Grove, IL: InterVarsity, 1973), 24.
5. Louw & Nida, *Greek-English Lexicon*.

God's sovereign direction in distributing gifts is also stated in Hebrews 2:4: "God also testified to it by signs, wonders and various miracles, and gifts of the Holy Spirit distributed according to his will." There is a sovereign plan, an eternal agenda that is being worked out by the Godhead. That plan includes partnering with mankind to accomplish the purpose of the living God. Holy Scripture reveals that God is directing his purpose by empowering his people to accomplish his goals by giving them spiritual assignments and the spiritual gifts to accomplish those assignments. Another term connected to this truth is grace, and it will be examined next.

The Gifts and Grace

There is a connection between the concept of grace and gifts. The two words come from the same root. The first is "grace" (χάρις) and the second is "gift" (χάρισμα). They connect the gift of God and the calling of God together. Paul writes to the Ephesians: "But to each one of us grace has been given as Christ apportioned it (Eph 4:7). This refers back to an earlier passage in the letter, where Paul links God's grace and his own calling and task as an apostle. "Although I am less than the least of all God's people, this grace was given me: to preach to the Gentiles the unsearchable riches of Christ" (Eph 3:8). Foulkes defines the term "grace" here and in Ephesians 3:2, 7, and 8 as, "the privilege of a special calling in the service of God."[6]

This concept is also expounded in 1 Peter 4:10 "Each one should use whatever gift he has received to serve others, faithfully administering God's grace in its various forms." The word "varied" (ποικίλος) here means, "pertaining to that which exists in a variety of kinds – of various kinds, diversified."[7] Here, again, is the richness of diversity represented in the body of Christ. The designed partnership between the Godhead and believers is also highlighted as mankind relates both vertically to God and horizontally to man. As the Holy Spirit distributes the gifts, each person has the responsibility to oversee it. The word "administering" (οἰκονόμος) means "one who has the authority and responsibility for something – 'one who is in charge of, one who is responsible for, administrator, manager.'"[8] D. E. Hiebert, in his

---

6. Francis Foulkes, *Ephesians,* trans. J. D. Emerson (Grand Rapids, MI: Eerdmans, 1956), 114.

7. Louw & Nida, *Greek-English Lexicon.*

8. Ibid.

commentary on First Peter, points out that the demonstrative adjective "each one" (ἕκαστος) stands emphatically first in the sentence, indicating that the task of steward has been given to each believer. The following word "just as" (καθὼς) points out that the service mentioned for each believer is determined and governed by the nature of the gift received. He goes on to say, "Each gift was bestowed for the purpose of 'ministering it among yourselves.' The reflexive pronoun (*Heautous*), as in verse 8, stresses the mutual benefit of the gifts when they are used for the benefit of the whole body. God has made the members interdependent; that which benefits others has a reflexive benefit for us."[9] The description of each believer as a steward is an important one. There is a distinction between an owner and a steward. In New Testament times, a steward was a person who was entrusted with property or wealth. They were to administer the assets according to the will of the owner. The steward was responsible to see that the owner's directions were carried out. In this verse the steward is to administer the gift given him for the benefit of those around him.[10]

Bruce comments on the concept of role and grace:

> Within the unity of the body each member has a distinct part to play, a distinctive service to perform, for the effective functioning of the whole. The ability to perform this service is here called the 'grace' given to each. Paul has referred above to the special 'grace' granted to him – the grace of apostleship (Eph 3:7–8), to be exercised not in any one local church but throughout the gentile world.[11]

There is a confluence of the purpose of God, the gifts of God, and the people of God as the Holy Spirit indwells believers and empowers them for their ordained role and ministry. Next is a brief look at the specific gifts mentioned in scripture.

The Gifts: A List

Erickson presents four major passages that list spiritual gifts: Romans 12:6–8, 1 Corinthians 12:4–11, Ephesians 4:11 and 1 Peter 4:11. Grudem would add

---

9. D. Edmond Hiebert, *First Peter* (Chicago, IL: Moody Press, 1984), 259.
10. Ibid., 259.
11. Bruce, *Colossians, to Philemon*, 339–340.

1 Corinthians 12:28 and 1 Corinthians 7:7. Both would agree that the lists recorded are not complete.[12] The lists themselves are different and are meant to reveal the variety of gifts that have been given by the Holy Spirit. Some gifts are described as an action, like "prophecy" (found in 1 Cor 12 and Rom 12), but also in a corresponding noun form, like "prophet" (such as in 1 Cor 12:28 and Eph 4:11). Paul, in his letter to the Corinthians, makes it clear that not every individual has all the gifts (1 Cor 12:29–30). He also makes it clear that all the gifts are necessary, no matter how unimportant or prominent they seem to be (1 Cor 12:22). The combined list of spiritual gifts is as follows:

1 Corinthians 12:28
1. apostle
2. prophet
3. teacher
4. miracles
5. kinds of healings
6. helps
7. administration
8. tongues

1 Corinthians 12:8–10
1. words of wisdom
2. words of knowledge
3. faith
4. gifts of healing
5. miracles
6. prophecy
7. distinguishing between spirits
8. tongues
9. interpretation of tongues

Ephesians 4:11
1. apostle
2. prophet

---

12. Erickson, *Christian Theology vol. 3*, 876; Grudem, *Systematic Theology*, 1019.

3. evangelist

   4. pastor-teacher

Romans 12:6–8

   1. prophecy

   2. serving

   3. teaching

   4. encouraging

   5. contributing

   6. leadership

   7. mercy

1 Corinthians 7:7

   1. marriage

   2. celibacy

1 Peter 4:11

   1. whoever speaks (covering several gifts)

   2. whoever renders service (covering several gifts)

As the world views men, women, and children from a multitude of backgrounds coming together in unity and purpose, they see the love of God demonstrated and the master plan of God revealed through his church. Grundem says:

> It runs counter to the world's way of thinking to say that we will enjoy greater unity when we join closely together with those who are different from us, but that is precisely the point that Paul makes in 1 Corinthians 12, demonstrating the glory of God's wisdom in not allowing anyone to have all the necessary gifts for the church, but in requiring us to depend upon each other for the proper functioning of the church.[13]

It is the Godhead's plan and pleasure that diversity and unity go together. The multifaceted wisdom behind the gifts is that God's purpose is fulfilled and that God's people would fulfill that purpose according to the core values of relationship and community. The next section looks in more detail at God's purpose for the gifts.

---

13. Grudem, *Systematic Theology*, 1022.

The Gifts: Their Purpose

The coming of the Holy Spirit and the works of the Spirit have long been in the mind of the Father. His sovereign plan has emerged throughout history. The Old Testament book of Joel, written hundreds of years before Christ, prophesied, "And afterward, I will pour out my Spirit on all people. Your sons and daughters will prophesy, your old men will dream dreams, your young men will see visions. Even on my servants, both men and women, I will pour out my Spirit in those days" (Joel 2:28-29). John the Baptist prophesied, "I baptize you with water for repentance. But after me will come one who is more powerful than I, whose sandals I am not fit to carry. He will baptize you with the Holy Spirit and with fire" (Matt 3:11). Jesus himself said, "Do not leave Jerusalem, but wait for the gift my Father promised, which you have heard me speak about. For John baptized with water, but in a few days you will be baptized with the Holy Spirit" (Acts 1:4-5). Pentecost ushered in a whole new spiritual dimension to the world. God's people became indwelt with the Holy Spirit and, as a result, were able to become partakers of the heavenly blessings. As part of God's family, they joined in the *missio Dei*.

The main purpose of spiritual gifts is to prepare God's people for works of service and for the building up of the church of Jesus Christ (1 Cor 14:5, 12, 26 and Eph 4:11-13). The Ephesians passage will be examined next.

> It was he who gave some to be apostles, some to be prophets, some to be evangelists, and some to be pastors and teachers, to prepare God's people for works of service, so that the body of Christ may be built up until we all reach unity in the faith and in the knowledge of the Son of God and become mature, attaining to the whole measure of the fullness of Christ. (Eph 4:11-13)

Many commentators, such as Bruce[14], Foulks[15], and Kent[16] see the phrases of verse 12 either as successive or as depending on the first phrase. There is a difference between the first preposition (πρὸς) and the following two (εἰς) that leads them to this conclusion. Therefore, there is an emphasis on the purpose stated: "to prepare God's people." The word for "prepare" is καταρτισμός: "to make someone completely adequate or sufficient for something – 'to make

---

14. Bruce, *Colossians, to Philemon*, 349.
15. Foulkes, *Ephesians*, 120.
16. Homer A. Kent, *Ephesians: The Glory of the Church* (Chicago, IL: Moody Press, 1971), 72.

adequate, to furnish completely, to cause to be fully qualified, adequacy.'"[17] There is a strong sense of God's direction and enabling here. Kent states, "The exercise of these Christ-given gifts was intended to coordinate and equip all believers for the work of ministry... Every believer, regardless of background, ability, or status, has a service to perform in the cause of Christ on earth."[18]

The Spiritual gifts, therefore, are for the purpose of enabling and empowering works of service and building up of the church. The Greek word for "build up" is οἰκοδομὴν. It has the meaning of "the construction of something, with focus on the event of building up or on the result of such an event – 'to build up, to construct, construction.'"[19] This same concept is stated by Paul to the church in Corinth, "So it is with you. Since you are eager to have spiritual gifts, try to excel in gifts that build up the church" (1 Cor 14:12).

The church is built up and members edified as each person functions according to their God-ordained gifts. The purpose of the gifts is to bring glory to the head, numerical growth to the body of Christ, and a supernatural unity seen by the world. Next we look at the scope of the gifts.

The Gifts: Their Scope

In examining the different types of gifts in the lists, it becomes clear that several different categories are revealed. The list in Ephesians deals with offices in the church or individuals who are God's gift to the church. In Romans and 1 Peter, basic functions are listed, while special abilities are listed in 1 Corinthians.[20]

As we consider the apostle Paul's two epistles, 1 Corinthians and Ephesians, the question is asked, "Who was his audience?" A second corresponding question is, "What would be the scope of the ministry of these gifts?" Are they limited to a particular house church, city church, a region, or the world? Concerning the recipients of 1 Corinthians, Paul begins his letter with, "To the church of God in Corinth, to those sanctified in Christ Jesus and called to be holy, together with all those everywhere who call on the name of our Lord Jesus Christ – their Lord and ours" (1 Cor 1:2). Paul addressed a specific local church and their specific problems and, at the same, time kept in mind the

---

17. Louw & Nida, *Greek-English Lexicon*.
18. Kent, *Ephesians*, 72.
19. Louw & Nida, *Greek-English Lexicon*.
20. Erickson, *Christian Theology vol. 3*, 875–876.

universal church as he wrote. Many of the themes of the letter were universal in nature. This is seen in the concept of the body of Christ that has been discussed above. In talking on 1 Corinthians 12, Radmacher states:

> In the process Paul makes it quite clear that the company comprehended within the "one body" is much more extensive than the local *ekklesia*. He does so, first of all, by including himself within the membership: "For by [en] one Spirit are we all [*hemeis pantes*] baptized into one body." Obviously this is not meant to assert that Paul had left his membership in the church at Corinth when he departed five or six years before.[21]

In the letter to the Ephesians, there is actually a discrepancy in the title. "The oldest manuscript of Ephesians that we possess, the Chester Beatty papyrus of about AD 200, and the great fourth-century codices Sinaiticus and Vaticanus, and certain other authorities do not have the words 'at Ephesus.'"[22] The lack of personal greetings in the letter adds to the theory that this was most likely an encyclical letter to churches that were geographically close to Ephesus.[23]

In discussing the scope of church as used by Paul in Ephesians, especially in association with the universal body of Christ, Radmacher states:

> In Ephesians and Colossians the word *ekklesia* occurs thirteen times and in only two instances (Col 4:15, 16) can the technical meaning be attached to it. Some things common to all of these eleven occurrences should be noted. In each case the word ekklesia occurs in the singular together with the definite article, which facts seem to give support to the one universal *ekklesia* absolutely.[24]

It seems clear that the epistles had a local and universal application. The very fact that we have a canon of Scripture to which Christendom refers demonstrates the timeless application of God's truths to all mankind throughout every generation. The individual believers in the local church at Corinth had gifts that were used in the context of that specific body. There

---

21. Radmacher, *What the Church*, 154–155.
22. Foulkes, *Ephesians*, 17.
23. Kent, *Ephesians*, 6.
24. Radmacher, *What the Church*, 156.

is a sense, as Hiebert stated above, that a specific gift is given to a specific person.²⁵

There are other ways of viewing the concept of gifts. Kenneth Berding would put the emphasis on the ministry one is called to, as opposed to the gift. Charles Van Engen would see the assigned ministry in the broadest context, not just a local church situation but a worldwide context.

In his book, *What Are Spiritual Gifts: Rethinking the Conventional View*, Kenneth Berding says he believes that the gifts are linked to ministries. Christ assigns ministries and then enables the individuals with the power and gifting to accomplish the ministry. He states:

> Let me begin with a summary. In this alternative approach, the so-called spiritual gifts are not special abilities; they're Spirit-given ministries. According to the contextual evidence in the letters of Paul, the so-called spiritual gifts should not be viewed as special abilities to do ministry; rather, they should be viewed as the ministries themselves. Every believer has been assigned by the Holy Spirit to specific positions and activities of service, small and large, short-term and long-term. These ministry assignments have been given by the Holy Spirit to individual believers and, in turn, these individuals in their ministries have been given as gifts to the church.²⁶

Charles Van Engen looks beyond the local setting and sees the working of gifts in the global context of *missio Dei*. As above, the focus shifts from the individual to almighty God, who is directing his people. He is not limited by the four walls of a church or by the local community geographically surrounding a church building. God views his people as one. He views his target group as all people in every country. Therefore, like a grand master of chess, he views the whole board and moves his pieces according to his sovereign plan, maximizing the abilities and unique qualities of each piece. Van Egan expounds:

> Although all this is familiar to us, we customarily associate the gifts of the Holy Spirit in this passage with individual persons as they live out their ministries in the context of a local congregation.

---

25. Hiebert, *First Peter*, 259.

26. Kenneth Berding, *What Are Spiritual Gifts: Rethinking the Conventional View* (Grand Rapids, MI: Kregel, 2006), 32.

However, given the global emphasis in the rest of the chapter, is it not legitimate also to apply Paul's concept of gifts here to the world Church? In that case, the passage would be telling us that in relation to the Church that surrounds the globe, some denominations and churches have certain gifts to offer, some mission boards have specific giftedness to bring, some one gift, some another.[27]

He continues:

A global hermeneutic of this passage has transformed the way I think of the gifts of the Holy Spirit. Now we are talking about each group of believers anywhere on the globe offering their gifts to all other believers anywhere on the globe. Now we conceptualize a Body of Christ whose members are spread throughout the entire world, dedicated to participating in Christ's mission of evangelizing the other four-and-a-half billion who yet do not know Jesus Christ as their personal Saviour and Lord. Each "member" of the global Body has something unique to offer the Body's ministry in the world. And, conversely, the Body is incomplete without the contribution of each member.[28]

There appears to be an element of truth in all the different emphases. The Godhead is directing the *missio Dei* and, therefore, the tasks assigned and the gifts given are intricately intertwined. The added perspective of Van Egan, which is to widen the scope of gifts/ministries from solely the local church context to include a global context, fits well with all learned so far in this study. There is recognition that God is the author of the ministries and the gifts as he sees fit. Each person views himself as part of a greater whole. Their particular role and gift cannot be seen as standing alone. Each gift and role is interconnected through the rule and enabling of the Holy Spirit, according to the purpose of the Father. That the Godhead partners with believers today to undertake ministry both locally and on a larger scale is clearly demonstrated through the teaching ministries of pastors such as Stewart Briscoe, John Piper, and Charles Swindoll, all of whom have had local and international ministries at the same time. God has ministered through their sermons at

---

27. Corwin and Mulholland, *Working Together*, 99.
28. Ibid., 100.

their churches, the books they have written, the seminars they have taught, and the international teaching engagements they have undertaken.

In looking at the world today, there are some significant individuals who have demonstrated the gift of evangelism. Luis Palau and Billy Graham are two of the most well known. Luis Palau has participated in hundreds of crusades in over seventy nations. In his decades of ministry, Billy Graham has been involved in a multitude of evangelistic outreaches. His crusades have reached over 200 million people in person and millions more through radio, TV, and film. He has preached in more than 80 countries around the world. He himself would say:

> "Why me Lord? Why did You choose a farm boy from North Carolina to preach to so many people, to have such a wonderful team of associates, and to have a part in what You were doing in the latter half of the twentieth century?" I have thought about that question a great deal, but I know also that only God knows the answer.[29]

It is clear in this example that God was in control. Only God could open the doors to so many countries, and, more importantly, only God could open the hearts of so many millions to receive his love. God designed it, called his servant and empowered him to accomplish his evangelistic purpose.

Summary and Reflection

The impact of the concept of Spiritual gifts on partnership in Christian missions is huge. The research has revealed that the Godhead is the source. The Holy Spirit determines who gets what gifts and the specific ministry in which those gifts will be used. It is all in accordance with the will and plan of the Father. Inherent within this is the understanding that each person has a part to play in the greater picture. No one person has all the gifts. By design there is an interconnectedness and interdependence. This is so that the focus is on God, not the individual. It demonstrates unity in diversity to a lost world. It forces individual believers to look beyond their own ministries and to the greater purpose of God. Spiritual gifts demonstrate the honor and responsibility of being a steward and partner with the Godhead in the purposes of God. The recognition of being part of the whole, under the

---

29. Billy Graham, *Just as I Am* (San Francisco, CA: Zondervan, 1997), 723.

leadership of the Godhead, should affect attitudes towards other believers as each one views the other as an important and intricate part of the whole that is ordained by God. This should generate a respect and honor amongst God's people, as well as an open desire to be used in conjunction with others as the Holy Spirit leads in the global purpose of the Living God.

In reflection, there is a growing understanding and acceptance of the concept of spiritual gifts within the partnership context. Personally, there has been growth in this area and progress made, but a new barrier has risen up that has impeded progress. I find that I have grown to recognize and appreciate various spiritual gifts as they are administered within my own familiar Western cultural context. However, I have not grown enough to recognize spiritual gifts as they are administered from a different cultural background; somehow the administration of those gifts seem wrong, out of place, or, at best, a "lesser" gifting. If my national brother has the gift of leadership, how does that work out in CARN council context? What does it look like? What about my Korean brother or Chinese sister? There needs to be a breakthrough in overcoming cultural bias as we recognize and welcome the administration of spiritual gifts in culturally diverse ways. May God open our eyes and hearts to his bountiful diversity and give us the ability to embrace all his ways.

In chapter 7, the concept of spiritual gifts and their use for the furtherance of the purposes of God were studied. They have been given by God and, by nature, foster interdependency amongst God's people. The last of the five theological issues chosen for this study that informs partnership is the church, both universal and local. The next chapter examines the relationship between the different Christian entities that make up the body of Christ. Historically, there has been difficulty in getting these entities to recognize one another and to work together. Discovering what Scripture teaches on "church" will help to break down barriers and encourage mutual respect and the ability to work together.

8

Partnership and the Church

Introduction

This chapter explores the relationship between the local and universal church as it relates to partnership in Christian mission. It begins with the Trinity and then continues on to explore the meaning of the word "church." The etymology and evolution of the word through the New Testament is traced. The pivotal passage of Acts 13 is examined to inform the local/universal discussion. Finally, the unique ministry context of the CAR is considered, along with one person's example of how partnership can happen at many different levels with many different entities.

The Church and the Trinity

The meaning of the word "church" (ἐκκλησία) is the focus of this section, and its first appearance in the New Testament is found in Matthew 16:18, where Jesus said, "I will build my church." It is a powerful and direct statement. It reveals his authority, purpose and connection to the forthcoming body of believers. This new assembly will carry his name and be characterized by his qualities. The church that Jesus will build is also described as being the church of God (Gal 1:13; Acts 20:28; 1 Cor 1:2; 10:32; 11:22). In Acts 20:28 the Godhead is pictured together in their unique roles. Paul had gathered together the leaders of the church in Ephesus and was giving them a farewell discourse. He exhorted them to mind themselves and to mind the flock, the people of God, for whom they were responsible. "Keep watch over yourselves and all the flock of which the Holy Spirit has made you overseers. Be shepherds of the church of God, which he bought with his own blood" (Acts 20:28). In this one verse the Triune God is portrayed in relationship with the church. It begins with the truth that the Holy Spirit assigns roles. The Holy Spirit himself has "appointed" (τίθημι - aorist middle indicative) the shepherds of the church. He has made these men "overseers" (ἐπισκόπους) of the flock. The body of believers is directly called the church of God. It exists through the purchase of the blood of God, the literal translation being "Which he bought with the blood of his own."[1] "His own" refers to the Lord Jesus Christ, as demonstrated in Romans 8:32: "He who did not spare his own Son, but gave him up for us all."[2]

Outside of the work of the Trinity, there is no church. Harper and Metzger explain:

> The church is a trinitarian community. For the church is the creation and covenantal companion of the God who exists as Father, Son, and Holy Spirit in eternal communion. The church belongs to the Triune God. The Father calls the church into being by the Son and indwells it by the Spirit, who unites it to Christ. The church is the people of God (1 Pet 2:10), the temple of the Holy Spirit (1 Cor 3:16), and the body and bride of Christ (Eph 5:29–32). Outside the Trinity, then, there is no church. For the people of God exist by way of the God, who elects it in the beloved and seals it by the Spirit (Eph 1:1–14). This relationship and sense of belonging determines the church's identity, purpose, and activity, and in that order.[3]

The Church: Definition of *Ekklesia*

The word "church" (ἐκκλησία) is a combination of the preposition *ek* "out of" and of *klesis*, which means "a calling." Some have pointed to this as proof that the church is a special called-out community. However, it seems best to agree with Radmacher and Louw and Nida that there is no warrant for this. The latter state:

---

1. John R. W. Stott, *The Message of Acts* (Leicester, England: IVP, 1990), 327.
2. I. Howard Marshall, *Acts* (Grand Rapids, MI: Eerdmans, 1980), 334.
3. Brad Harper and Paul Louis Metzger, *Exploring Ecclesiology: An Evangelical and Ecumenical Introduction* (Grand Rapids, MI: Brazos Press, 2009), 19.

Though some persons have tried to see in the term ἐκκλησία a more or less literal meaning of 'called-out ones,' this type of etymologizing is not warranted either by the meaning of ἐκκλησία in NT times or even by its earlier usage. The term ἐκκλησία was in common usage for several hundred years before the Christian era and was used to refer to an assembly of persons constituted by well-defined membership. In general Greek usage it was normally a socio-political entity based upon citizenship in a city-state.[4]

Therefore, the word carried the meaning for ancient Greeks of an assembly of people who had been summoned. Vine comments on its Old Testament usage: "In the Septuagint it is used to designate the gathering of Israel, summoned for any definite purpose, or a gathering regarded as representative of the whole nation."[5]

Baur lists four ways in which the word was used in the Greek-speaking world:[6]

1) *assembly*, as a regularly summoned political body . . .

2) *assemblage*, gathering, meeting . . .

3) *the congregation* of the Israelites, esp. when gathered for religious purposes . . .

4) of the Christian *church* or *congregation* . . .

This last category can be divided into several specific meanings. It can be used simply as a church meeting, as the church or congregation, as house churches, and as the church universal to which all believers belong.[7]

The common secular usage of the word is demonstrated in Scripture in the book of Acts. The place was Ephesus, and there was a riot surrounding the gospel ministry and the Apostle Paul. The Ephesians gathered in the theatre and chanted for two hours "Great is Artemis of the Ephesians" (Acts 19:34). Three times, this unruly crowd was referred to as "the assembly" (ἡ ἐκκλησία) (Acts 19:32, 39, 41).

---

4. Louw & Nida, *Greek-English Lexicon*.
5. Vine, *Expository Dictionary*, 84.
6. Baur, *Greek-English Lexicon*, 240.
7. Ibid.

The word started to take on a special meaning during the time of the apostles. It became identified as a certain kind of assembly. It was associated with the One who said he would build his church. Those gathered in these assemblies came with a Christian identity and unity. The word "assembly" took on this new content and became associated with the spiritual characteristics of the people gathered.[8]

The word for "church is used in a variety of ways throughout the New Testament. Radmacher gives an overview of its distribution, "According to Moulton and Geden there are one hundred and fourteen occurrences of *ekklesia* in the New Testament."[9] It is worthwhile to examine the different ways the word is used in order to understand the different potential entities that could join in collaboration together for a common goal as God directs.

The Church: Forms of *Ekklesia*

"Ekklesia" has a rich and varied application as it refers to believers in the many different situations in which they exist. The term never refers to a building or denomination but always represents people who have been saved by grace. The first reference is to those who are found to be in Christ wherever they are in the world.

Ekklesia as All Believers

Within Scripture there is a major use of the word "the church" in the singular form. It does not refer to a small house group or local assembly of any kind. It refers, instead, to all who would call on the name of Jesus around the world. Radmacher states:

> The doctrine of the universal church arises out of an inductive study and systematization of the metaphorical usages of *ekklesia* in the New Testament. When the apostle Paul comes to the metaphorical use of the *ekklesia* (predominately in Ephesians and Colossians), he conceives of an entire world of individual Christians immediately related to Christ apart from local *ekklesiai*, and he terms them simply the (only) *ekklesia*. Thus, the concept of the physical assembly gives way to the spiritual

---

8. Radmacher, *What the Church*, 1380.
9. Ibid., 133.

assembly. The locative of place yields to the locative of sphere (*en Christo*).¹⁰

The universal church is revealed through the metaphor of "the body of Christ" in which Jesus is the head. "And he is the head of the body, the church; he is the beginning and the firstborn from among the dead, so that in everything he might have the supremacy" (Col 1:18). The church is seen as the recipient of his sacrificial death: "Christ loved the church and gave himself up for her" (Gal 5:25). The universal church reflects the concepts studied already in previous chapters concerning the body of Christ and the unity of the one people of God. There cannot be two churches of Jesus Christ. There cannot be two brides; otherwise Christ would be torn asunder.¹¹ Grudem summarizes well:

> We may conclude that the group of God's people considered at any level from local to universal may rightly be called "a church." We should not make the mistake of saying that only a church meeting in houses expresses the true nature of the church, or only a church considered at a city-wide level can rightly be called a church, or only the church universal can rightly be called by the name "church." Rather, the community of God's people considered at any level can be rightly called a church.¹²

These are people who are in community under the name of Jesus Christ. They are people who are linked to Christ and to one another. There is recognition that this community is a vast universal community comprising those in every city, country, and region around the world and, at the same time, the people worshiping and interacting in a local house church. Shelly explains:

> The New Testament teaches that all those who are brought by faith into a new relationship with Christ find themselves thereby brought into a new relationship with a host of others. The sense of being Christ's brings with it, immediately and inseparably, a sense of oneness with all Christ's people. On the broad scale, this is a confessional community, since it is based on a common confession, made by lip and life, that Jesus is Lord. On a narrower

---

10. Ibid., 187.
11. Ibid., 194–195.
12. Grudem, *Systematic Theology*, 857–858.

scale, it is a local Community, since the believer finds himself actually meeting together with those living in his vicinity who profess this same faith – loyalty to Jesus Christ. So when New Testament writers speak of the church (ekklesia), they always do so in one or the other of these two senses. And frequently we can't separate sharply the two senses.[13]

Below are several attempts at defining the church.

Erickson:

"The whole body of those who through Christ's death have been savingly reconciled to God and have received new life. It includes all such persons, whether in heaven or on earth. While it is universal in nature, it finds expression in local groupings of believers which display the same qualities as does the body of Christ as a whole."[14]

Grudem:

"The church is the community of all true believers for all time."[15]

Clowney:

"According to the Bible, the church is the people of God, the assembly and body of Christ, and the fellowship of the Holy Spirit."[16]

Only God knows those that are truly his. Those who are found in Christ make up his church regardless of where they live or who they are in association with. The vast majority will be found in community with others, however, there will be those who are isolated, not by their own choice but by the circumstances surrounding them. Scripture has revealed the world wide body of Christ. It also refers to those within a specific geographical region as the church.

---

13. Bruce L. Shelly, *What Is the Church?* (Wheaton, IL: Victor Books, 1978), 15.
14. Erickson, *Christian Theology vol. 3*, 1034.
15. Grudem, *Systematic Theology*, 853.
16. Edmund P. Clowney, *The Church* (Downers Grove, IL: Intervarsity, 1995), 28.

Ekklesia *as All Believers in a Region*

Paul writes to the churches in Galatia, "Paul, an apostle – sent not from men nor by man, but by Jesus Christ and God the Father, who raised him from the dead and all the brothers with me, To the churches in Galatia" (Gal 1:1–2). Galatia was a Roman province of Asia Minor. Although there has been some discussion as to the recipients being from the northern or southern districts, the fact remains that many local churches existed in this region, and Paul addressed them as "churches."[17] Paul addresses the "churches" (plural) of the region. At the same time, the New Testament sees the churches in a region as the "church" (singular). This is seen in Acts 9:31: "Then the church throughout Judea, Galilee and Samaria enjoyed a time of peace. It was strengthened; and encouraged by the Holy Spirit, it grew in numbers, living in the fear of the Lord." This "church" (singular) had been ravaged by a young man named Saul. He testifies how he persecuted the church. Paul admits, "For you have heard of my previous way of life in Judaism, how intensely I persecuted the church of God and tried to destroy it" (Gal 1:13).

The church of God in a region has been described above. The regional church can be broken down to smaller units – those who reside in a specific city. The church, viewed in the context of a city, is explored next.

Ekklesia *as All Believers in a City*

The first four chapters of Acts record the enormous growth in the church in Jerusalem; thousands came to faith in those first weeks (Acts 2:41; 4:4). The people of God were spread over the whole city. They met together in many separate houses. This was true in many of the large cities where the gospel produced much fruit. The conglomeration of many house churches in one city was also called collectively "the church" (singular identity). All of the believers of the various house churches of Jerusalem were called "the church" (Acts 11:22). The same is true for Ephesus (Acts 20:17), Antioch (Acts 11:26), and Laodicea (Col 4:16). It is worthwhile to examine one of these cities, Antioch, to be able to understand the diversity of the people of God in that city. Antioch was a large city of some 500,000 people. It was the capitol of Syria and ranked only behind Rome and Alexandria as the largest city in the Roman Empire. The Jewish community had grown for three

---

17. Robert H. Gundry, *A Survey of the New Testament* (Grand Rapids, MI: Zondervan, 1981), 248.

hundred years and numbered around 25,000.[18] The gospel was first carried to this Jewish community as a result of the scattering of believers due to the persecution after Stephen's martyrdom (Acts 8:1). This community of Jews most likely lived in a "Jewish quarter." The gospel spread amongst them for ten years before it took hold in the Gentile community, which represented the remaining 475,000 people of the city. Wagner states:

> The Antioch churches were all house churches or neighborhood churches. How many of the Antioch Gentile people groups such as those of the Syrians, Greeks, Romans or any number of others had networks of house churches growing among them we do not know. But whatever the number, the rule among them, with very few exceptions, if any, would be that the people who met regularly in any of the neighborhood house churches would have lived near each other and been from the same people group.[19]

To call the believers in Antioch "the Church" demonstrates the unity and diversity of the body of Christ. It was a culturally mixed group inclusive of many separate house fellowships. The next reference refers to those small local house churches that make up the bulk of the number of the uses of the word church.

Ekklesia as a Single Local Gathering

There were no church buildings in the time of the apostles. There were no venues that could hold hundreds or thousands of people for the purpose of worshiping the Lord Jesus Christ. Instead, those in the first days met in the synagogues, or, for the Gentiles, they met in the homes of individuals. This is seen clearly in Paul's epistles as he gives special greetings to the Saints. "Give my greetings to the brothers at Laodicea, and to Nympha and the church in her house (Col 4:15). "Greet Priscilla and Aquila, my fellow workers in Christ Jesus. They risked their lives for me. Not only I but all the churches of the Gentiles are grateful to them. Greet also the church that meets at their house" (Rom 16:3–5).

House churches were the normal setting for the growing body of Christ in each of the cities. Paul uses ἐκκλησία to describe these intimate, small

---

18. C. Peter Wagner, *Lighting the World* (Ventura, CA: Regal Books, 1995), 91–92.
19. Ibid., 144.

assemblies that gathered for the purpose of worshiping and following the Lord Jesus Christ.

It is clear that there are various ways to define and describe the church, depending on the emphasis or specific focus. When it comes to the issue of missions, there has been much debate as to the relationship between the local and universal church when it comes to the practical outworking of strategy, authority, and accountability. This next section addresses that issue, which is key to understanding how God's people can work together on behalf of the lost in a specific region or for a specific people group.

The Church: Local versus Universal Debate

The discussion concerning the role and authority of the local church versus the universal church, as reflected in mission agencies and organizations, has been going on for decades. The questions are "Who has authority, and who is in charge?" The very same questions exist today in the CAR. Individuals are asking, "How does it all fit together?" Others are demanding that any mission activity must be under the authority and direction of a local church. So, the main question of who is in charge needs to be addressed.

Background of the Debate

There has been much discussion in the post-World-War-Two-years about the relationship between the church local and the church universal. This has been spurred on by the proliferation of non-local church "entities," such as Youth with a Mission, Campus Crusade for Christ, Young Life, InterVarsity, Operation Mobilization, and thousands of other groups. It also reflects the relationship between emerging or established national churches and the remaining mission organizations or denominations that birthed them. The discussion has focused on: the emerging national church versus the parent foreign mission church, denomination verses denomination, one local church verses other local churches, the local church verses mission organizations, and the list goes on. This issue is central to the concept of partnership in missions in CAR. There has been tension and division in the body of Christ over how the local church and universal church interact and work together.

Lausanne Discussion of the Debate

At the Lausanne congress in Pataya in 1980, this issue was examined. It turned out to be an emotional and pertinent topic. As a result, a commission was formed to further explore the issues and gather the research into a paper to present to the Lausanne committee. The result in 1983 was the *Lausanne Occasional Paper #24*, titled "Cooperating in World Evangelization: A Handbook on Church/Para-Church Relationships." As the committee met over several weeks and considered the need for world evangelism in the context of the local/universal church problem, they all agreed that a special function needed a special organization. The heart of the debate was, "Who should initiate it? Who should operate it?"[20]

Some of the main issues that the committee outlined which hindered the relationship between the local church and what they called the para-church included:[21]

1) Dogmatism about non-essentials and differing scriptural interpretations (matters of theology, conviction, terminology, tolerance)

2) The threat of conflicting authorities (matters of validity, mandate, accountability, fear)

3) The harmfulness of strained relationships (matters of attitude, prejudice, personality, fellowship)

4) The rivalry between ministries (matters of goals, duplication, specialization)

5) The suspicion about finances (matters of fund raising, publicity, overhead, overseas aid)

There were some who felt that non-local church entities had no right to exist. Others saw them as not biblical but still used of God. John Stott summarized the situation concerning these "para-church" entities in the preamble to *LOP 24* this way, "Independence of the church is bad, cooperation with the church is better, service as an arm of the church is best."[22]

Ralph Winter, in trying to address this issue years earlier, set out the concept of sodalities and modalities. He strove to demonstrate that, from the

---

20. "Cooperating in World Evangelization," *LOP* 24, 6.
21. Ibid., 12–13.
22. Ibid., 6.

earliest chapters of Acts, throughout church history, and up to the present day of mission organizations, God has used both the local church (modalities) and missionary bands (sodalities) for his glory and for the accomplishment of his purposes. Winter states:

> Thus, on the one hand, the structure we call the *New Testament Church* is a prototype of all subsequent Christian fellowships where old and young, male and female are gathered together as normal biological families in aggregate. On the other hand, Paul's *missionary band* can be considered a prototype of all subsequent missionary endeavors organized out of committed, experienced workers who affiliated themselves as a second decision beyond membership in the first structure. Note well the *additional* commitment. Note also that the structure that resulted was something definitely more than the extended out reach of the Antioch church. No matter what we think the structure was, we know that it was not simply the Antioch church operating at a distance from its home base. It was something else, something different.[23]

As the different sides took their stand, one of the major battlegrounds for this discussion was Acts 13. Some claimed that the primary initiator of missions was the local church in Antioch, while others stated it was the missionary band. Therefore, a look at the passage is key.

A Key Text in the Debate (Acts 13)

The main debate centers around Acts 13:1–4, where Paul and Barnabas are sent out from Antioch. However, the story begins long before the Holy Spirit spoke to those who were gathered in that city. It is addressed in Paul's encounter with Jesus on the Damascus road and, before that, in eternity past, in the mind of the Godhead. God intervenes in the course of history as the Lord Jesus confronts the religious fanatic, Saul, on his way to imprison believers in the city of Damascus. Luke recounts the story:

> As he neared Damascus on his journey, suddenly a light from heaven flashed around him. He fell to the ground and heard

---

23. Ralph D. Winter, "The Two Structures of God's Redemptive Mission," *Perspectives on the World Christian Movement: A Reader,* 4th ed. 1981 (Pasadena, CA: William Carey Library, 2009), 245.

a voice say to him, "Saul, Saul, why do you persecute me?" "Who are you, Lord?" Saul asked. "I am Jesus, whom you are persecuting," he replied. "Now get up and go into the city, and you will be told what you must do. (Acts 9:3–6)

The religious community is about to be turned upside down. Saul's reputation had preceded him to Damascus. There was fear in the Christian community, as this man had the power and authority to ruin their lives and throw them into prison. While Jesus intervened in Paul's life, he also intervened in the life of a local believer in Damascus named Ananias. The Lord supernaturally revealed his will to his servant, Ananias. He commanded him to go to Saul and to pray for him. Ananias initially balked at the idea because of Saul's reputation (Acts 9:13). At that time the Lord revealed his sovereign plan for the future. It concerned Saul, specifically, and part of his salvation plan for the Gentiles. "But the Lord said to Ananias, 'Go! This man is my chosen instrument to carry my name before the Gentiles and their kings and before the people of Israel. I will show him how much he must suffer for my name'" (Acts 9:15–16). Included with the prediction of the future ministry is also the future suffering that Saul will endure.

The idea of ministry to the Gentiles was formed in the mind of God before the creation of the world. Paul later, in Acts 13, acknowledges the calling and command of God on his life. It was long in the mind of God to reach the Gentiles, and Paul connects his present ministry with the words of the prophet Isaiah:

> For this is what the Lord has commanded us: "I have made you a light for the Gentiles, that you may bring salvation to the ends of the earth." When the Gentiles heard this, they were glad and honored the word of the Lord; and all who were appointed for eternal life believed. The word of the Lord spread through the whole region. (Acts 13:47–49)

God, as the author of salvation, singled out Paul for his specific task and part in the *missio Dei*. It was not Paul's or anyone else's idea. He states this in his letter to the Galatians, "Paul, an apostle – sent not from men nor by man, but by Jesus Christ and God the Father" (Gal 1:1).

In his testimony before King Agripa, Paul gives a fuller account of what the Lord Jesus said to him as he outlined his future ministry. Jesus said to Paul:

> Now get up and stand on your feet. I have appeared to you to appoint you as a servant and as a witness of what you have seen

of me and what I will show you. I will rescue you from your own people and from the Gentiles. I am sending you to them to open their eyes and turn them from darkness to light, and from the power of Satan to God, so that they may receive forgiveness of sins and a place among those who are sanctified by faith in me. (Acts 26:16–18)

It is within this context, of the predetermined purpose of God for the man Paul, that the passage of Acts 13 must be interpreted:

In the church at Antioch there were prophets and teachers: Barnabas, Simeon called Niger, Lucius of Cyrene, Manaen (who had been brought up with Herod the tetrarch) and Saul. While they were worshiping the Lord and fasting, the Holy Spirit said, "Set apart for me Barnabas and Saul for the work to which I have called them." So after they had fasted and prayed, they placed their hands on them and sent them off. The two of them, sent on their way by the Holy Spirit, went down to Seleucia and sailed from there to Cyprus. (Acts 13:1–4)

The nature of the church of Antioch has already been discussed above. It was a huge cosmopolitan setting, and the church in the city was made up of smaller house groups. These groups contained both Messianic fellowships and Gentile fellowships. Luke lists five people who were present in the meeting when the Holy Spirit supernaturally intervened and gave the Godhead's command. John Stott gives the background of these five:

The cosmopolitan population of Antioch was reflected in the membership of its church, and indeed in its leadership, which consisted of five resident *prophets* and *teachers*. Luke explains neither how he understood the distinction between these ministries, nor whether all five men exercised both or (as some have suggested) the first three were prophets and the last two teachers. What he does tell us is their names. The first was *Barnabas*, whom he has earlier described as "a Levite from Cyprus" (4:36). Secondly, there was *Simeon* (a Hebrew name) called Niger ("black") who was presumably a black African, and just conceivably none other than Simon of Cyrene who carried the cross for Jesus and who must have become a believer, since his sons Alexander and Rufus were known to the Christian community. The third leader, *Lucius* of *Cyrene*, definitely came from North Africa, but the conjecture of some early church fathers that Luke was referring to himself is extremely improbable, since he carefully preserves his anonymity throughout the book. Fourthly, there was *Manaen*, who is called in the Greek the *syntrophos* of Herod the tetrarch, that is, of Herod Antipas, son of Herod the Great. The word may mean that Manaen was "brought up with" him in a general way, or more particularly that he was his "foster-brother" or "intimate friend." In either case, since Luke knew a lot about Herod's court and family, Manaen may well have been his informant. The fifth church leader was *Saul*, who of course came from Tarsus in Cilicia. These five men, therefore, symbolized the ethnic and cultural diversity of Antioch.[24]

It is important to comment that none of these five men were native to Antioch; each of them had come from the outside. In this sense, none of these leaders were indigenous to the city. The other important fact is that, of the five, none of them is said to be an elder.[25] They are called "prophets" (προφῆται) and "teachers" (διδάσκαλοι). In light of the fact that the church was vast in Antioch, the meeting in which the Holy Spirit appeared and gave direction must have been some type of a smaller gathering. A detailed description of the meeting and who was present is not given beyond the five men listed. Luke just records that "In the church at Antioch there were . . ." He is referring to all the believers in the city. It is inappropriate to picture this as a typical Western scenario of the First Baptist Church on Main Street, with the pastor, elders and entire congregation present. Some, such as Wagner, see this meeting as a gathering of foreign missionaries that have come to Antioch to work with the Gentile community and to plant Gentile churches.[26] What the real situation was, we do not know, but this was a unique group. While they were worshiping, God intervened. The Holy Spirit initiated the whole episode. An imperative is given to those in the meeting to "set apart" (ἀφορίζω) Paul and Barnabas. The meaning of this word is "to set aside a person for a particular task or function."[27] The work is something that the Holy Spirit has called them specifically to do. From the information gleaned

---

24. Stott, *Message of Acts*, 216.
25. Wagner, *Lighting the World*, 146.
26. Ibid., 148.
27. Louw & Nida, *Greek-English Lexicon*.

from Acts 11 concerning Paul's future ministry, it seems that the time had come to begin this new phase. It was in line with the timing, purpose and will of God. This is emphatically expressed again several verses later, as the inspired Luke repeats that it was the Holy Spirit that sent them on their way (Acts 13:4). Gooding summarizes:

> It was very natural, then, that the men whom God had appointed as prophets and teachers should together wait on God for him to show them how they should set about the vast task of preaching to the Gentiles and teaching them the doctrines of the Christian faith. And it was likewise very natural that men sent out by the Holy Spirit on this great task were chosen from these prophets and teachers. It is often so. It is the men who have been given the gift, rather than the church at large, who have the vision both of the need and of the way that need should be met. Happy the men who in that situation have the confidence, blessing and backing of their church in the work to which the Holy Spirit (not the church), sends them (13:4).[28]

The beauty and richness of the family of God is revealed in the timing and method of the Holy Spirit delivering the command to Paul and Barnabas. The task had already been assigned before this meeting. God chose that exact moment, with exactly those present, to give the command to start. They were together in community with others. They were in a time of worship and fasting in community with the living God. God included the Antioch church as he assigned his agenda to Paul and Barnabas. Having lived and ministered together for over one year (Acts 11:25–26), they were family. God would include them all in his plan. There was agreement amongst all present about their calling and joint obedience, as the Antioch church released them, blessed them, and sent them on their way. The church did not initiate the mission trip; they responded in obedience to the direct command of the Holy Spirit. They joined with God in the mission that was assigned for two people they loved. They would be committed to pray for them as they left in obedience to go where the Spirit would lead them. When the missionary journey was completed, it was with great joy and excitement that Paul and Barnabas returned to their Antioch family and shared what God had done.

---

28. David Gooding, *True to the Faith: A Fresh Approach to the Acts of the Apostles* (London: Hodder & Stoughton, 1990), 208.

> From Attalia they sailed back to Antioch, where they had been committed to the grace of God for the work they had now completed. On arriving there, they gathered the church together and reported all that God had done through them and how he had opened the door of faith to the Gentiles. And they stayed there a long time with the disciples. (Acts 14:26–28)

This strong relationship and collaboration in the purpose of God continued as Paul embarked on his second missionary trip with Silas. He had been in Antioch quite a while, and, when he departed, he had the blessing and commendation of the brethren there: "but Paul chose Silas and left, commended by the brothers to the grace of the Lord" (Acts 15:40). The word "commended" (παραδίδωμι) means "placed under the protective power of the grace of God."[29] The brethren in Antioch committed Paul and Silas in God's hands as they departed to revisit the places from the first missionary journey.

The sending out of this first missionary band was a significant milestone in the unfolding story of the book of Acts. As close and connected as Paul and Barnabas were to the church in Antioch, there is not a strategic or oversight function of the church recorded. Actually, just the opposite is the case. In Appendix A of *LOP 24*, those attesting to the autonomy of Paul's missionary band state:

> More than one missiologist felt this passage to be not only a strong biblical basis for the organizing of mission sodalities, but the very "hinge of mission history." It is pointed out that the Holy Spirit guided the apostolic band (Acts 13:4; 16:7). The leaders of the band mapped out their own course (18:23), and the missionaries themselves chose the methods and planned the strategy as the Holy Spirit led them (19:21). Approval was not sought from Jerusalem or Antioch (cp., Acts 15). The missionaries recruited en route (16:3) and even in Antioch (15:36–41). Personal problems (again, 15:36–41) were hammered out by the band members; and there was no evidence of financial help from Antioch (see 1 Cor 9:18).[30]

---

29. Colin Brown, ed. *The New International Dictionary of New Testament Theology, Vol. II* (Grand Rapids, MI: Zondervan, 1971), 368.

30. "Cooperating," *LOP* 24, 45.

Acts 13 reveals that God, in his sovereignty, called and appointed Paul to his Gentile mission. He did this while Paul was in fellowship with prophets and teachers in Antioch. The Holy Spirit commanded the group to join in this calling and release Paul and Barnabas for the task to which they had been called. There was obedience from Paul and Barnabas and from the Antioch believers to do what the Spirit commanded. This now leads to the answer of our original question.

The Answer to the Debate

The initial issue that was raised at the beginning of *LOP 24* was simply, "Who should initiate it? Who should operate it?" It seems clear, through the research done so far, that the answer is simply "God." God initiates it, and God oversees it. The Holy Trinity is working in relationship. The Godhead has the plan, determines the roles, the strategies, and the giftings. God is the one in control – not any one local church or denomination, not the mission agency, and not the individual. He uses people and churches and organizations as he chooses. He alone is the master planner. He alone can match Paul to serve with Barnabas. He alone can call them while they are in relationship with the brethren in Antioch. He alone can include those in Antioch to join in the praying and sending. God does not relinquish control over his plan and purposes. He calls on his people in many shapes and forms to partner with him. White summarizes:

> Both the local church and the para-local church groups comprise vital and viable parts of the body of Christ. The para-local church finds its theological legitimacy in the freedom of form given in the New Testament, in the necessary expression of each believer-priest in his ministry, and in the examples of local and mobile functions of the universal church. The local church is God's basic medium for meeting the broad needs of people of all ages and in all situations. The mobile para-local church structure is God's method for the two-fold task of missions and specialized ministries.[31]

The focus is on God. In today's world, he has more resources than ever before in history to call on to join him in his sovereign plan for redeeming

---

31. James R. White, *The Forgotten Trinity* (Minneapolis, MN: Bethany House, 1998), 85.

mankind. He is no longer restricted to believers in Judea and Samaria, but he now has a global body that he is directing and empowering for his purpose. For the last 1,400 years, there has basically been no visible indigenous church in the CAR. However, God is mobilizing his worldwide body on behalf of the national people in CAR. The following is a present-day picture of the reality on the ground and how God is orchestrating, in fresh and exciting ways, his people in all their structures for his task, blending local and universal forms of his church.

The Church in All Its Forms in the CAR

It is important to place theological reflection within a given context. This study has as its context the CAR. It is a unique place in terms of the church of Jesus Christ. There are four major issues that dominate the context of the CAR in the twenty-first century. They are: the present influx of Christian media, the persecution and oppression of Christianity by the dominant religion, the cosmopolitan nature of the CAR states, and the emerging mission movements targeting the CAR. These issues impact partnership in Christian missions in CAR. The Lausanne covenant on the church and evangelism declares "the whole church taking the whole gospel to the whole world."[32] It appears that the whole world is coming to CAR, and, therefore, a better understanding of what the church looks like is necessary in order to inform partnership in missions. Several charts will be presented to highlight the different aspects of the body of Christ in CAR.

Koivisto's View of the Universal Church

A helpful chart by Rex Koivisto (Chart B) paints a solid picture of what the Universal Church looks like.[33] The larger circle represents the Universal Church or the community of all believers everywhere. Most are in community with others, but some are not. The churches are both independent and part of denominations and are connected graphically by being on the outer line of the circle. Koivisto points out that churches are made up of a mixed community. Only God knows who really belongs to him, so local churches

---

32. "Lausanne Covenant", <http://www.lausanne.org/covenant> (14 April 2010).
33. Rex A. Koivisto, *One Lord, One Faith: A Theology for Cross-Denominational Renewal* (Eugene, OR: Wipf and Stock, 1993), 271.

have both believers and non-believers in their make up. This chart is a good starting point, but it limits individual believers to being isolated or part of a traditional local church.

Chart B: Koivisto's View of the Universal Church

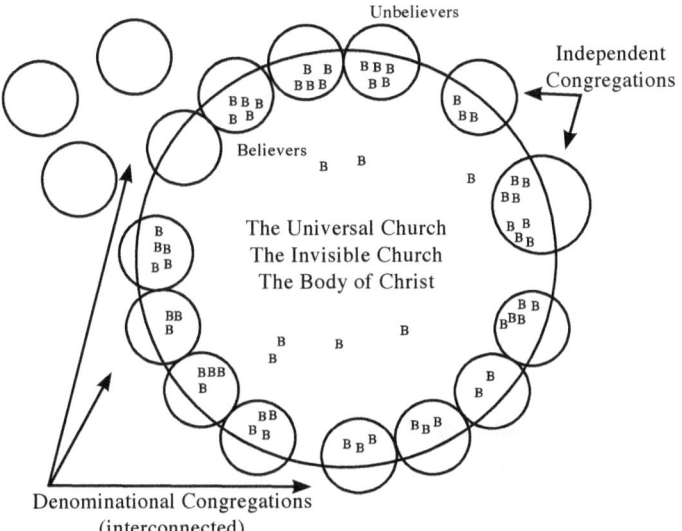

In the CAR context, the picture is a bit more complex than just the two categories above. The next charts focus in on specific situations within the CAR, beginning with indigenous believers.

Indigenous Believers in the CAR

This study deals with Partnership in Christian missions, and, therefore, the focus is on those indigenous people within CAR who have never heard the gospel. One of the major goals for partnership in mission is to see these individuals reached for Christ.

Chart C: Individual Believers Connected Outside the CAR

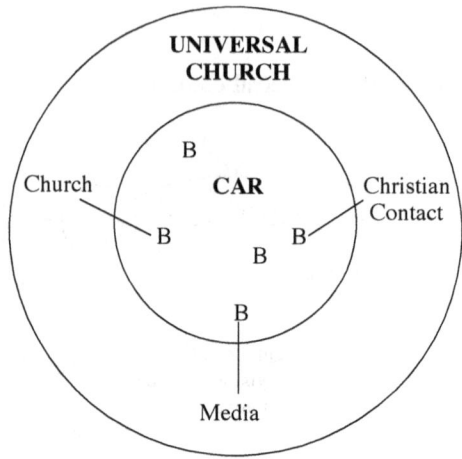

Presently, there are scattered believers throughout the region. Chart C reflects the unique nature of these believers, represented by the letter B. Some stand totally alone and isolated; they have come to faith through a dream, vision, radio, etc., but they have no connection with other believers. Another category of B has studied overseas, come to faith, and has a vital connection with a church in another country. That church is their remote family; they phone, skype and write as they are able. Another B is connected with a media ministry; this could be through the Internet, a TV program, or radio. All of these ministries have follow-up programs, and for some B's this is the only connection they have to other believers. The uniqueness is that, in these days, media ministries realize that believers in closed countries, who cannot be open about their faith for fear of death, are looking to them for their community and relationship. They text, call, and write to the program, and key individuals disciple and fellowship with them; they develop close personal relationships. Other B's represent those who have met a Christian on an overseas trip; they have remained in contact and come to faith. Their connection is with that one other believer. Intense persecution and opposition has forced creative solutions to the needs for fellowship and discipleship. In the present CAR scenario, community in some situations is seen in a way other than sitting in a room together with other believers. The next chart focuses on the more traditional local church.

Local Churches in the CAR

Chart D: Local Churches in the CAR

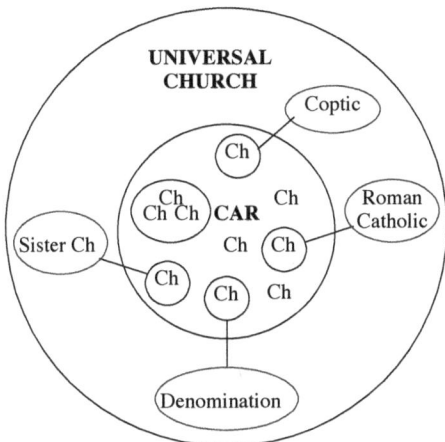

Chart D focuses on the status of local churches in CAR. With the expatriate population so high (one city in the CAR is over 90% expatriate), there are multiple denominations and churches represented in CAR. Some local churches relate outside to a mother denomination; this would include churches like the Anglican, Marthoma, Syrian Orthodox, Coptic, Reformed, Roman Catholic, and a myriad of other smaller Indian and Filipino denominations. Besides these, there are dozens of local independent churches that stand alone and have no connection or relationship outside or inside CAR. This would also include secret fellowships of indigenous believers meeting in homes. Then there are autonomous churches that have formed into loose networks. The Evangelical Church in one CAR country would fall in this category. It would have some thirty-plus churches of all different nationalities and languages, joined by a common doctrinal statement and constitution, yet with no connections with any outside denomination. Within the CAR there are expatriate churches in each country made up of expatriate Christian-background nationals from nearby countries. The point of this chart is to highlight the vast diversity of the local churches in the CAR. The next chart looks at the complete body of Christ in the CAR.

The Church in the CAR

Chart E: The Church in the CAR

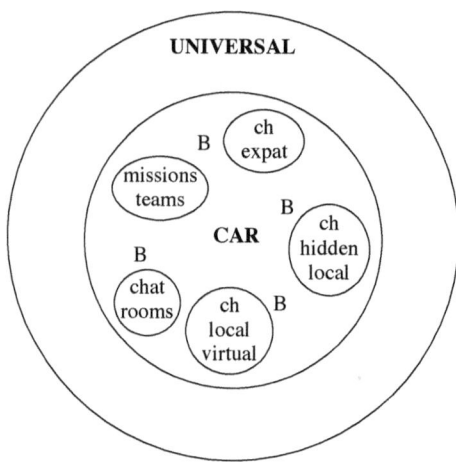

Chart E seeks to represent the composition of the body of Christ in the CAR. The body of Christ is made up of secret believers, secret house churches, open house churches, denominational churches, local virtual fellowships through the Internet, and isolated believers. The focused missionary teams are an important addition to this mix. These teams are found in places where there is no known local church, such as in three of the CAR countries. Members of the teams come from different countries, sponsored by different home churches, and sometimes belong to different mission agencies. Yet, on the ground they worship together, share the Word together, baptize new believers together, and partake of communion together. The body of Christ is diverse in this unique non-Christian setting. The next chart gives a picture of the multiple types of ministries targeting the CAR.

Universal Church's Impact on the CAR

Chart F: Universal Church's Impact on the CAR

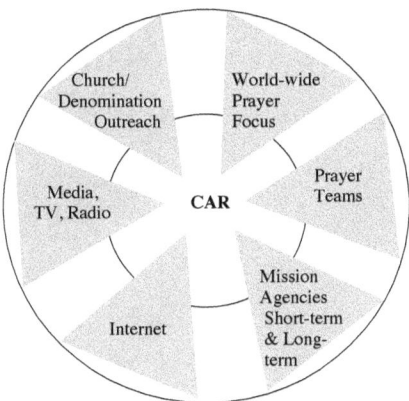

The world has changed greatly in just the last twenty years. The emergence of the Global South, the Internet, and a fresh new worldwide missions vision have all helped to make for a new and unique situation. Chart F represents the focused missionary efforts that are concentrated on the CAR in these days. These are all ministries that are coming from outside of the region, hoping to engage the peoples of the CAR with the gospel. The different ministries that are targeting the CAR include:

- Denominations – New ones are coming all the time with their diverse ministry visions.
- Internet – Every year there are more and more sites that offer chat rooms, programs, discipleship etc.
- Media – Thirteen years ago, there was only one CAR-language Christian channel on satellite TV; now there are at least seven. Radio continues to beam into the region with its various programs targeting specific language groups.
- Prayer/Evangelism Teams – These are coming for a week to one month from countries around the world. They come to have an impact and to share the gospel. They desire to create a long-term vision for the country in those who go.
- Mission agencies – In the last twenty years, the number of missionaries with agencies has grown from around 50 to 500. New

mission agencies are coming, especially from countries like Nigeria, Indonesia, the Philippines, South Africa, and Latin America.

Chart F highlights the diversity and complexity of the worldwide body of Christ as it seeks to impact the CAR for Christ. The last chart attempts to portray the big picture of partnership in light of all that has been studied concerning the Trinity, the church, and ministry.

Chart G: Partnership Examples in the CAR

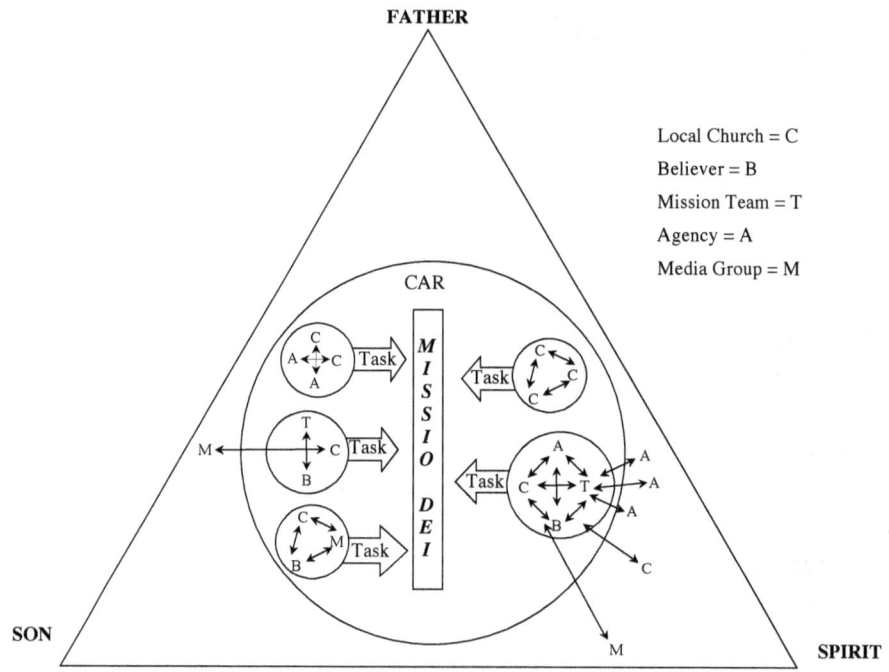

Partnership in the CAR

Task is important. God has called his people to partner with him to do something. Chart G reflects that it is the Triune God who is in charge and accomplishing the *missio Dei*. One segment of God's world is the CAR. It is a unique region, with its own specific context and challenges. God, in his sovereignty, is raising up people both inside of CAR and outside to impact those indigenous inhabitants of CAR who have not heard of the gospel. To accomplish his purposes, his people are brought together in creative and special ways. Some groupings are large, and some are small. It could be two families joining together in ministry in their neighborhood, or it could be something like the CAR Consultation. Chart G gives several possible examples. Task is often what brings people together who otherwise, in their normal state of affairs, would not have had contact. As God's people are brought together, their relationship with one another becomes crucial as they work together to accomplish the task before them (John 17).

Having looked at the incredible complexity and diversity in the CAR, it becomes clear that only God can do it. God is calling people, churches, and organizations from places like Holland, Canada, Brazil, Indonesia, Nigeria, China, and South Africa to join with him in his purpose to reach the lost of the CAR, just as he called Paul from Antioch. He uses sodalities and modalities. The time is now for the CAR. God is calling on his people to follow his leading. He is calling on them to use their gifts in the roles he has decreed. He is calling on them to partner with those he chooses for the accomplishment of his purposes.

We need to be partnership people. Working in the midst of both modalities and sodalities can be confusing. However, being part of the body of Christ, in its various forms, is a rich and precious privilege. Here is one man's experience in working and ministering within different entities.

The Church: A Practical Example

How does this blending of local and universal church work itself out in a practical way on the ground? I submit one man's experience as a positive example. He has worn three hats, and each role overlaps with the others. He has been a leader of an organization, involved in a Network (a partnership of many different missions agencies and churches) that is working on behalf of a region. He was also a pastor-at-large with an International church in that region.

He was originally the interim pastor for the International Church and served in that capacity for a year until another pastor was found. He has a profound love and respect for the local church. He remained a member of the church and used his gifts of teaching and preaching over the years. As a member of the church, he placed himself under the authority of the Elders. When asked to preach, it was under their direction. There was submission to the leadership of the church; this was his relationship with his local church. Even though he held "pastor" status with the Evangelical Church in the country, he was a mission leader and partnership leader for the region. When it came to fellowshipping in his local church, there was respect and honor for the leadership and their role in the kingdom of God. They, in turn, set him free to minister around the region and the world as God gave open doors. Besides his local church in this city, he also had strong links with fellowships back in his home country. These churches prayed for him, supported him, and were involved to various extents in his life. There was a strong bond between these churches and him. One church was invited to be part of the decision-making council for his mission agency's work in the region.

Besides the personal long-term link with home churches, there are the hundreds of local churches in dozens of countries around the world where he has preached and shared about the ministry in his region. As the family of God, there was an instant connection, a rejoicing in what God was doing. As a missionary, there was respect for him as their guest and for his role in the kingdom of God. There was submission from his part as he entered their community and tried to fit into what God was doing locally, whether that promoted his region or not.

As a mission leader, he found himself not operating in a vacuum but in community with the rest of the body of Christ in the region. Because he was linked with the Evangelical Church in that country, he came under their authority, as well. As a mission organization, he would confer with the others before attempting a "risky" evangelistic project. He would submit to the group if they thought it not wise. At times, he would use his contacts and influence to host events that would directly benefit the local expatriate churches in the nation. Sometimes these events did not directly have anything to do with evangelism of the indigenous peoples, but they were building up the body of Christ.

As a facilitator in the regional network, he realized that the relationship between mission agencies was key. The regional partnership was formed because he believed in the unity of God's people and also that together they could accomplish more. In the various countries, joint teams were formed, joint projects undertaken, and even joint fundraising accomplished. Their attitude as a partnership was that they were part of the one body of Christ. They had their strengths that they used as God directed, and they collaborated with others as he opened the door. They encouraged participation from individuals, local churches, denominations, and mission agencies, both inside and outside the region, to work in partnership as the Holy Spirit directed opportunities. They recognized that God is in charge of ministry to the nationals in the region.

Summary and Reflection

This chapter began, as all the others, with the primacy of the Holy Trinity. Acts 28:13 demonstrated the relationship of the Godhead with the church. The Triune God, throughout the study, has been the central theme, along with the concepts of community and relationship. The crucial concept of church was unpacked to reveal its meaning as house, city, region and universal. Concerning the conflict of who is in charge between the local and universal church, the conclusion was that God is in charge; he is in control. He directs his body, determines strategies, and empowers and gives gifts to his people. He is working today through his universal church to accomplish his redeeming purpose in the CAR. He expects his people to be partnership people – those who live in community and relationship with him and with one another and who, when instructed to do so, obediently work closely together in unity for his glory.

In reflection, one of the great privileges of my life has been that God has allowed me to see with my own eyes how he has been working through local churches, denominations, mission agencies, and individuals for his glory and purpose around the world. Most Christians have not had this privilege. They know mostly their own context, and, therefore, see others as outsiders; the universal church is only a theory, not a life experience for them. If they only knew, if they only had contact, they would taste and see that the Lord is good in other contexts beside their own. What has become natural for me is still an unknown for many. May God open our eyes to the richness of his body and our part in it.

This chapter brings to a close the archival study on the biblical and theological themes that inform partnership in missions. The next chapter listens to the community of the CAR Consultation as they respond and reflect on the five areas studied thus far and contribute to the understanding of partnership in Christian missions in CAR.

9

Survey Results and Analysis

Introduction

This chapter outlines the results from the survey (in the Appendix) that was given to the attendees of CAR Consultation held in November 2009. It lists the individual responses to each question according to the information matrix. It then describes the demographic information of the attendees and analyzes the answers to the open-ended question.

Survey Overview

The objective of the survey was to have input from CARN community in regard to the five theological themes that were considered key to a theology of partnership in Christian missions. The theological themes needed to be tested within CARN community because that is where the meaning and application of partnership will be lived out. There was overwhelming agreement amongst the delegates of CARC on the questions asked relating theological issues to partnership in CAR. The results of the survey will be displayed through the use of seven tables representing the responses and four charts demonstrating the demographics of those involved in the survey.

The survey responses were skewed positively, so much so that the median and mode for questions 1–20 and 22 were all 7. Question 21 was inverted, and the median and mode for it was 1. The distinction between a normal distribution and the results of this survey are represented in Chart H:

Chart H: Distribution Comparison

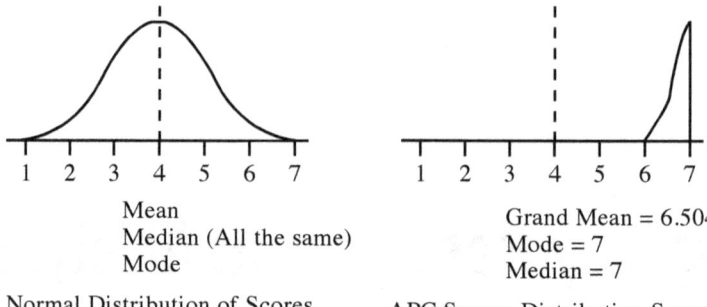

Traditionally, one would examine variability on the Likert scale scores using the interquartile range. Due to the homogeneity of the responses and the leptokurtic positively skewed distributions, the computation of the interquartile range was not appropriate. Therefore, the data can best be analyzed by simply observing the frequency distribution tables and reflecting on possible reasons for the results. The bottom line is that, statistically, the median and mode are identical. Therefore, the results indicate that there is incredibly strong agreement in all the responses. The next section examines the tables of response scores.

Tables of Response Scores

The first table (Table 3) takes a look at the frequency distribution of all the responses. The next table (Table 4) addresses the grand tour questions, and each table after that is grouped around one of the five theological themes. The numbered questions are in order of the intended flow from Objective Knowledge to Subjective Knowledge to Attitude to Behavior on each theological theme.

Table 3: Frequency Distribution for Questions 1–22

Frequency Distribution of Responses for Questions One to Twenty-two
(205 Total Respondents)

Question #	No Answer	1	2	3	4	5	6	7	Median	Mode
1	1	0	0	0	0	0	5	199	7	7
2	1	2	1	5	8	14	18	156	7	7
3	0	0	0	2	2	1	6	194	7	7
4	1	0	0	1	2	12	29	160	7	7
5	2	4	0	3	5	11	12	168	7	7
6	1	5	1	7	15	25	30	121	7	7
7	1	0	1	4	6	16	35	142	7	7
8	1	1	5	6	10	18	23	141	7	7
9	1	0	0	0	5	23	35	141	7	7
10	1	4	2	4	15	16	33	130	7	7
11	2	4	3	2	14	23	31	126	7	7
12	1	1	2	2	3	15	35	146	7	7
13	0	1	2	3	3	16	37	143	7	7
14	1	1	2	2	1	1	20	177	7	7
15	1	0	0	1	3	16	33	151	7	7
16	0	0	0	0	2	23	42	138	7	7
17	2	0	0	0	0	4	9	190	7	7
18	3	0	2	0	3	24	36	137	7	7
19	3	0	2	0	5	18	34	143	7	7
20	3	3	3	4	9	24	29	130	7	7
21	1	131	36	15	8	5	3	6	1	1
22	5	5	3	6	13	19	38	116	7	7

Table 3 gives the frequency distribution of the responses for all twenty-two questions. The results from a statistical standpoint are positively skewed. There are several factors that most likely lead to these results. First, CARN is an evangelical network. The CARN has adopted the Lausanne Statement of Faith. This was to be expected on the objective theology questions. Second, the majority of people present (70%) belong to evangelical organizations. Their theological background would be similar, and their exposure to working with others would be at a high level. Third, the number of people present at CARC who had been there before was 53 percent; therefore, their exposure to and acceptance of partnership principles is reflected in their responses. Fourth, CARC is known as a partnership event where information is shared and networking takes place. Therefore, those who come would have already embraced general partnership ideas. Fifth, there has been a growing global focus on partnership in missions. This has resulted in more agencies and churches desiring to work together. The number of strategic partnerships around the world has grown radically since the mid-1980s. Phill Butler lists the existence of one partnership in 1986, with ninety in 2002.[1] Regional networks have grown, such as AWEMA in the Middle East, SEALINK in South East Asia, COMIBAM in Latin America, and MANI in Africa. Sixth, in Christian circles the idea of partnership has become more accepted. There is a general understanding that Christians should love one another and work together even if the reason for that belief cannot be articulated in detail. This could explain the high positive response from the 47 percent of people who were first time attendees of CARC.

Table 4: Grand Tour

Frequency Distribution of Responses for Grand Tour Questions

Question #	No Answer	1	2	3	4	5	6	7	Median	Mode
6	1	5	1	7	15	25	30	121	7	7
20	3	3	3	4	9	24	29	130	7	7

Table 4 shows the frequency distribution of responses to the "Grand Tour" questions. The concept behind these two questions was to give a "big-picture" question concerning partnership for people to interact with. They were not included within the five theological themes matrix but meant to stand alone. Question #6 had the most comments directed toward it from the open-ended opportunity. In general, people believe in partnership but not without some limitations. These limitations will be addressed in the section on the open-ended responses.

Table 5: Trinity

Frequency Distribution of Responses Related to the Theological Theme of TRINITY

Question Type	Question #	No Answer	1	2	3	4	5	6	7	Median	Mode
Knowledge-Objective	1	1	0	0	0	0	0	5	199	7	7
Knowledge-Subjective	8	1	1	5	6	10	18	23	141	7	7
Attitude	11	2	4	3	2	14	23	31	126	7	7
Behavior	4	1	0	0	1	2	12	29	160	7	7

The fifth table reflects the responses on the first theological theme, that of the Trinity. The doctrine of the Trinity was the highest rating with 199 out of

---

1. Phill Butler, "A Survey of Kingdom Collaboration," *Mission Frontiers Magazine*, May–June 2006, 13.

205 responding a 7. There was a slight decrease in the number of respondents to question #8. This question had the second highest number of referrals in the open-ended question section. For a few, it was a bit of a jump to move from "the Trinity working together" to "people working together." This is reflected even more in question #11; there is a slight difference for some between the doctrine of the Trinity and how that should impact partnership.

Table 6: Mission

Frequency Distribution of Responses Related to the Theological Theme of MISSION

Question Type	Question #	No Answer	1	2	3	4	5	6	7	Median	Mode
Knowledge-Objective	5	2	4	0	3	5	11	12	168	7	7
Knowledge-Subjective	7	1	0	1	4	6	16	35	142	7	7
Attitude	15	1	0	0	1	3	16	33	151	7	7
Behavior	9	1	0	0	0	5	23	35	141	7	7

Table 6 deals with the mission of God. There was strong overall agreement to missions being God's plan. However, it is interesting that four people strongly disagreed to this statement. They were all Westerners. None of them commented in the open-ended question. I would love to talk to these people and explore their responses more.

Table 7: Body

Frequency Distribution of Responses Related to the Theological Theme of BODY

Question Type	Question #	No Answer	1	2	3	4	5	6	7	Median	Mode
Knowledge-Objective	3	0	0	0	2	2	1	6	194	7	7
Knowledge-Subjective	12	1	1	2	2	3	15	35	146	7	7
Attitude	13	0	1	2	3	3	16	37	143	7	7
Behavior	19	3	0	2	0	5	18	34	143	7	7

Table 7 deals with the body of Christ. Next to the Trinity, it had the highest score of agreement. The scores were clustered together quite closely for the knowledge, attitude and behavior questions. Again, there was a slight decrease in those who rated the objective truth (194) as compared to the others (143). I believe that individuals' concern about limitations or boundaries is the cause for this difference. However, the median and mode were still seven, showing a very strong agreement to the concept.

Table 8: Gifts

Frequency Distribution of Responses Related to the Theological Theme of GIFTS

Question Type	Question #	No Answer	1	2	3	4	5	6	7	Median	Mode
Knowledge-Objective	14	1	1	2	2	1	1	20	177	7	7
Knowledge-Subjective	22	5	5	3	6	13	19	38	116	7	7
Attitude	18	3	0	2	0	3	24	36	137	7	7
Behavior	16	0	0	0	0	2	23	42	138	7	7

Table 8 deals with the gifts of the Spirit. There was not as much agreement going from the objective statement that the Holy Spirit is the source of our gifts to using them in conjunction with others for missions. This particular score was the lowest in the survey in terms of maximum agreement. This was an interesting result, when there are passages, revealed in the archival research, that clearly present the Holy Spirit as the source and distributor of gifts.

Table 9: Church

Frequency Distribution of Responses Related to the Theological Theme of CHURCH

Question Type	Question #	No Answer	1	2	3	4	5	6	7	Median	Mode
Knowledge-Objective	17	2	0	0	0	0	4	9	190	7	7
Knowledge-Subjective	10	1	4	2	4	15	16	33	130	7	7
Attitude	2	1	2	1	5	8	14	18	156	7	7
Behavior	21	1	131	36	15	8	5	3	6	7	7

Table 9 deals with the church, local and universal. As with the Trinity, there was an overwhelming agreement to the doctrine of the universal church. There were sixty less people that translated that doctrine to "working together because we are one body." The response to question 21 was a bit disturbing, as it seems there was an intentionality of a few to actually choose to not work with other evangelicals outside of their church or organization.

It was personally encouraging to see this level of agreement in the overall survey results. The next section looks at the demographics of CARC attendees.

Demographic Information

The demographic data gathered in the survey came from four questions. These dealt with the delegates' representation, home continent, current residence, and if this was their first attendance or not.

Delegate's Representation

Chart I: Representation

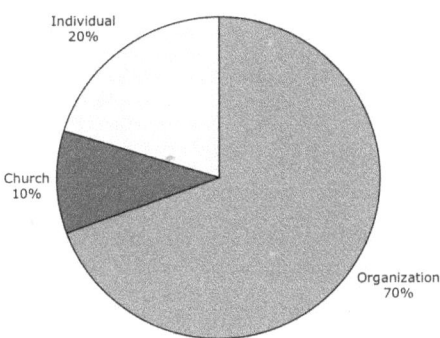

Chart I shows whether the delegates came as representatives of their church or organization or as an individual. Each year the participation in CARC varies to some extent. In 2009, 70 percent of the delegates stated that their main affiliation in relationship to this consultation was with their organization. Individuals that came of their own accord, as in contrast to being sent by a church or an organization, represented twenty percent of the total attendees. Finally, those representing a specific local church or denomination were 10 percent

Delegates' Home Base by Continents

Chart J: Delegates' Home Continents

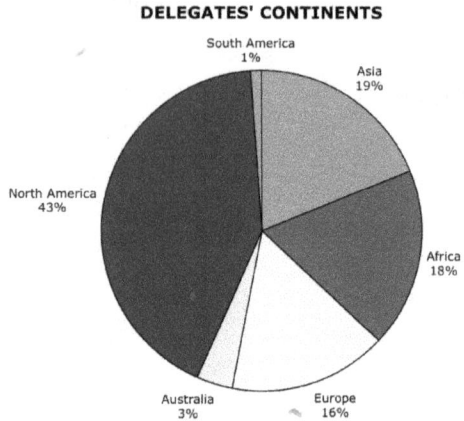

Chart J delineates where each delegate comes from originally. The majority of attendees (57%) were not from North America (43%). This represents a reflection of the growing interest in missions from the Global South into the CAR. Over the last three years, there has been a large push by CARN council to include Asians and Africans in CAR Network. Koreans and Chinese make up the majority of Asians, with Nigerians and Egyptians the majority of Africans in attendance. The high percentage of North Americans reflects the number of organizations with North American roots, which includes organizational leaders present and also the high number of North American workers on the field.

Delegates' Residence

Chart K: Where Delegates Live

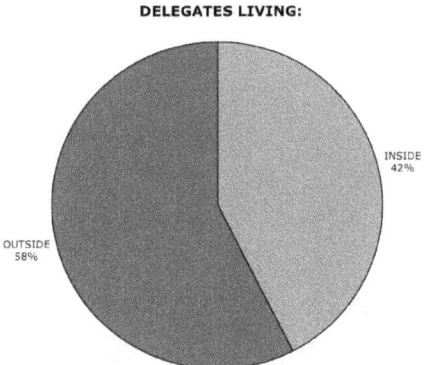

Chart K simply reflects if people live within the countries of CAR or outside. Those from outside CAR were 58 percent, and those living inside were 42 percent. The original design of CARC was to be able to give people from around the world an opportunity to visit and see how they could join in ministry to the peoples of the region. The program is designed to give an overview of the countries and allow people from the outside to interact with those working on the ground. These numbers reflect the intent in the original design of CARC.

First Time Attendees

Chart L: First Time Attendees

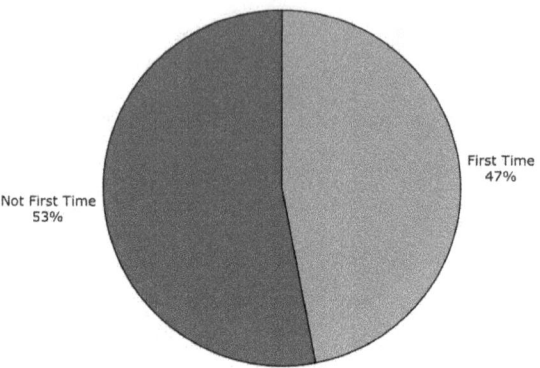

Chart L reflects the question "Is this your first CARC?" This statistic was an eye opener. One would have thought that the number of returning delegates would have been quite a bit higher than the first-time comers. However, the ratio is 53 percent who had attended before and 47 percent who were attending for the first time. Negatively, one could ask where those are who had come in the past? Was it not worth their while to come again? Positively, the word is spreading, and more people are interested and making the effort in both time and money to attend a consultation on CAR.

Open-Ended Questions

Forty-one people out of the 205 took advantage of the open-ended question opportunity. These comments can be divided up into a few main categories. There were those who gave a general "well done" or "thank you" for the partnership event. Several others made the point that partnership is a result of the priority of people loving others and each individual's obedience to Christ. There were five responders who did not like the survey. They felt it was: "flawed through emotionally charged questions"; "many questions are loaded"; "poorly worded"; and "seemed to be a set up survey intended to come to a conclusion (fore decided)." A few others felt that the definitions were not clear or that they were encountering a new doctrinal idea in relation to partnership. One particular person, in responding to the Godhead working together as a model for partnership, said, "I haven't thought of that."

The most helpful comments came as people spoke of the need for partnership and the limitations of partnership. Concerning the need for partnership, people responded that: (1) The present CAR and neighboring regions context of spiritual openness dictates partnership; (2) The workers are few and the need so great; (3) The need to glorify Christ through unity and mutual respect; (4) Working in partnership to reflect the body of Christ and to avoid waste and duplication; and (5) Working in partnership will help in reaching the nations. Concerning the limitations, the most comments came in the area of putting some boundaries around the idea of partnership. Each person said partnership was good but that there were limitations to working together. The limitations are listed below :

1) Sometimes God calls a lone evangelist to the desert. There are exceptions to always working together.

2) There is a biblical exhortation to partnership however if individuals have not awakened to that concept yet they are not in an "unbiblical" state.

3) Although partnership is good God does not force it.

4) There can be good reasons why it is not always possible or appropriate to work in partnerships.

5) God does tend to lead individuals into pioneering ministries, thus alone.

6) Doctrinal beliefs dictate different levels of partnership.

7) Unity in partnership does not mean uniformity.

8) People work with those who share the same vision/calling.

9) The level of operational security, or lack of security, can hinder partnership even though the desire is there.

10) Not sure that unity is equal to partnership.

11) Cultural and organizational differences can hinder partnership and adversely effect joint goals.

12) Unity in the body of Christ is key yet there are times when sin, compromise, syncretism dictates a limitation to partnership.

13) Terms of partnership are important. It is not unbiblical to not work with some Christians with whom one does not agree on basic gospel ministry elements.

The feedback from the open-ended question was helpful. It allowed me to understand more of what people were thinking. The issues mentioned were not new to me, with the exception of security (#9 above). It was encouraging that people were thinking through the area of limitations.

Summary

The interaction of the CARC attendees with the five theological issues was a learning experience. It was not too surprising that there was such strong agreement on the objective doctrinal statements, such as "the scriptures teach that God is one in three." The overall agreement with the rest of the questions represented in the median and mode being seven was surprising. I thought there would have been a little more disagreement than there was. Within the results there was a bit of a difference between what a few people believed and what they actually did. Some of this could to be the result of not transferring knowledge of the Godhead working together into action of people working together as they are doing God's business. The other aspect of the survey was the voice of those who mentioned limitations in partnering together. Not everyone works together all the time in every situation with everyone else. The issue of limitations in partnership is a significant one. There could be one hundred percent agreement on the theological reasons to partner together, but if one group uses unsecured communication that would endanger another in a closed access country, then that other group may chose to distance themselves.

One of the more exciting results was the number of first-time attendees (47%), which reflects a growing interest in ministry to nationals in the CAR. It also reflects that the first-time attendees to the CARC were in agreement with the five theological issues presented in the survey. There was no significant difference in the responses in their theological agreement concerning partnership between those who had been to the CARC before and those who were first-timers. Another exciting thing was the diverse nature of the group with people from almost every continent on earth.

Overall, it was good to see that the CARC community was in agreement with the importance of the five theological themes as they related to partnership in the CAR. The final chapter reflects on all that has been discovered through this study and its application to the CAR context.

10

Conclusions and Recommendations

Introduction

Writing in 1955, Max Warren, began his book with the words "Partnership is an idea whose time has not yet fully come."[1] It has been over fifty years since that statement, and I believe he would rejoice in the state of missions today. Partnership is not just an unreachable goal talked about at major conferences but an actual fact of the missions experience today.

Conclusions

In the CAR we have had a working partnership for sixteen years. It is small in comparison to the overall total number of Christians present in the CAR, but it has been active and highly successful. The CAR Network is geographically growing in every direction. People are coming from around the world to see how they can partner with others for the sake of the lost in the CAR. As encouraging as this is, we also realize that the vast majority of evangelical believers living and working in the CAR are not connected with those outside of their local church or with the CAR Network. Many have no concept of sharing the gospel with the indigenous people or of working together with other groups or churches to reach their own people. There is still a long way to go for God's people to be mobilized for missions and to be engaged in fruitful partnership for the sake of the gospel. The exact reasons for this lack of partnership activity are unclear. The literature review of this study

---

1. Warren, *Partnership*, 11.

has shown that there are various barriers to overcome to enable people to work together in partnership. Issues such as culture, establishing joint vision, conflict resolution, and developing trust are just a few that were mentioned. It is hoped that this study, which focuses solely on the theological issues, will have a positive and encouraging impact on those in this category, leading towards deeper relationships in collaboration for the gospel.

The purpose of this study was to conduct research towards the formulation of a missiological theology of partnership in Christian missions in the CAR context in order that the body of Christ may be encouraged to greater cooperation in the accomplishment of the Great Commission. This study revealed that God in three Persons is the ultimate reality. The Triune God dwells in community, love, and relationship. It has always been that way and will continue for eternity. Mankind has been invited to join this God in a personal relationship. It is only within this relationship with the living God that there is significance and life. God created mankind for this relationship with himself. Heaven is described as an eternal state where believers dwell in the presence of Almighty God face-to-face. Unfortunately, as recorded in Genesis chapter 3, the perfect relationship established between God and man was broken. The mission of God revealed in Scriptures is to restore the relationship with man. The Bible, from Genesis to Revelation, unpacks that mission. God, in his sovereignty, chose to include man in his plan and to give to man the message of reconciliation. As God drew mankind to himself through the death and resurrection of Jesus Christ, he included them into his family. He filled them with his Holy Spirit and gave them gifts through his grace for service in his eternal plan. He has established a role and mission for each one according to his desire. He has given a code of behavior to his people. He has called on them to be and act as family, in unity and love together. This unity is extremely important. It demonstrates to a lost world that Jesus came from the Father. Each believer is part of God's family. Each believer is called to live in obedience to the Father. Each believer is interconnected to the greater family of God. Each person is given a role and gift to fit into the sovereign mission of God. These are the theological truths revealed in the study. In light of these truths, each person, church, or agency has the ability and calling to:

- Give praise to God for his love.
- Love others because God loves them.
- Freely submit to his Lordship and direction.
- Rejoice in other believers, churches, agencies and their calling and gifting.

- Joyfully enter into specific partnerships with others.
- Invest time in relationships.
- Rest and be content in the role and gift that God has given.
- Recognize that those from other cultures and countries are part of the family.
- Share abundantly with others the gifts given by the Holy Spirit.
- Seek out Spirit-inspired new relationships.
- Trust God that he will accomplish his task in and through them
- Trust God that he will accomplish his task in and through others.

Understanding partnership in Christian mission begins with the recognition and acceptance of the truths outlined above. Each person, local church, denomination, mission agency is a part of the whole. Therefore, partnership in the CAR is the unique opportunities in working with the Triune God and the body of Christ to accomplish the *missio Dei* under the power and direction of the Holy Spirit.

The two questions stated at the beginning of this dissertation that were to guide the research were:

1) What specific theological issues inform partnership in Christian missions in the CAR?

2) How do workers in the CAR interact with those theological issues?

The first question has been covered above. The second was found in the results of the CARC survey. The field research clearly showed that there was strong agreement from the CARC community on the theological issues and their impact on partnership. The survey community included 96 first-time attendees (out of 205 total). This demonstrates that there is agreement to the theological issues from people who have not been associated with CARC. It leads one to believe (although not proven) that there is wide acceptance of these theological issues in the worldwide missions community. Therefore, the CARC community has confirmed this study, which has demonstrated through the archival research that there is strong biblical support for the concept of partnership.

As professed in my adopted definition of theology stated in chapter 1, it has been my desire through this study to understand the character, will, and acts of the Triune God concerning partnership in missions as he has revealed them in Scripture and to formulate these in a systematic way in order that we in the CAR might know him, learn to think our thoughts after him, live our lives according to these truths, and, by our thought and action, project his truth into our relationships and our ministries here in the CAR. On a personal note, this study has changed my life. It has changed the way I view myself. Every day, I see myself in relationship, first with The Triune God and then with his people. I am truly part of a greater whole. I see others as created in God's image, gifted, called, and appointed to be part of God's *missio Dei*. I have a new respect and honor for all I meet, along with a new desire for community and ministering in unity. I have a fresh recognition and joy in the richness of the diversity of God's people. I have gained a clearer understanding of "why" I do partnership.

Recommendations for Future Studies

During the course of the study, several issues for future research and future projects became apparent. From the beginning, it was recognized that this study was only a piece of the puzzle in working towards a theology of partnership. First of all was the concept of relationships. The relationships explored for this study primarily came from Paul's life. The reason for this was because of the partnership language that he employed. It would be good to examine the Old Testament for similar relationships and to gain a richer and broader understanding of relational principles that inform partnership. Second, the concept of heaven was very intriguing. It would be good to do a thorough study on heaven, focusing on the relational principles there that should have an impact on collaboration today. Third, I believe that prayer is the key to missions. It is the untapped power of Christians. There needs to be more research on the interconnectedness of prayer as it relates to the Godhead, the task, and the believers involved. Fourth, for the specific context of the CAR, it would be good to do a survey of the mission agencies involved in the region. Since there is strong theological agreement, based on the CARC survey, it would be good to explore what, in their view, are the limitations or barriers to even more collaboration taking place. Fifth, since the survey was limited to those in CARC, it would be significant to do a survey using the same questionnaire, giving it to some of the local expatriate churches and tentmaker teams who have not been involved in the CARN, and see if there is any significant differences in the responses to the theological themes or any enlightening statements in the area of limitations. Finally, as the issue of limitations was significant in the survey responses, it would also be good for a future study to explore any "limitations" in the biblical materials. By this, I mean what perceived examples in Scripture (such as some of the OT prophets or Paul and Barnabas' disagreement over Mark) would be exceptions or put a different light on the idea that God's plan is always for people to work in relationship together to accomplish his purposes.

In conclusion, my desire for this study in my life and others is found in Christ's high priestly prayer, "My prayer is not for them alone. I pray also for those who will believe in me through their message, that all of them may be one, Father, just as you are in me and I am in you. May they also be in us so that the world may believe that you have sent me" (John 17:20–21). The ultimate goal is that we would be in unity and that many more would come into a saving relationship with the living God.

Appendix

CARN Survey

As a participant in CARN family, your input is valued as we strive to learn more together about partnership in the CAR context. By "mission partnership" we mean "Gods people working together to accomplish God's purposes." The results of this survey will be included in the doctoral dissertation on "A Theology of Partnership in CAR." All surveys are confidential, and the results will be available at the next CARC in 2010.

DIRECTIONS: Please circle the number that best represents your view along the scale mentioned for each specific area. Thank you for your participation in carefully reading and responding!

Question/Statement	Response (circle your rating)
1. The Scripture teaches that God is One in Three: three distinct Persons, one God.	Disagree = 1 < > Agree =7 1 2 3 4 5 6 7
2. Local churches and mission groups are equal partners in mission partnership.	Disagree = 1 < > Agree =7 1 2 3 4 5 6 7
3. The Scripture teaches that all who believe in Jesus Christ as Savior are included in the one "Body of Christ."	Disagree = 1 < > Agree =7 1 2 3 4 5 6 7
4. Have you pursued personal friendship relationships with those outside your organization or church?	Never=1 < > Always=7 1 2 3 4 5 6 7
5. The Scripture teaches that mission is essentially God's Work: His idea, His plan, His effort.	Disagree = 1 < > Agree =7 1 2 3 4 5 6 7
6. If we do not work together in partnership, we are un-Biblical.	Disagree = 1 < > Agree =7 1 2 3 4 5 6 7

7. Since mission is essentially the working out of the One God's plan, we must work together in mission partnership.	Disagree = 1 < > Agree =7 1 2 3 4 5 6 7
8. Since the Persons of the Trinity work together in saving us we should also work together in mission partnership.	Disagree = 1 < > Agree =7 1 2 3 4 5 6 7
9. Have you taken an active part in a partnership project when appropriate?	Never=1 < > Always=7 1 2 3 4 5 6 7
10. Since all Christian groups are included in the one Body of Christ, they must work together in mission partnership.	Disagree = 1 < > Agree =7 1 2 3 4 5 6 7
11. The model of the Godhead working together to save us inspires you to work intentionally in mission partnership.	Disagree = 1 < > Agree =7 1 2 3 4 5 6 7
12. Since we are one "Body of Christ," we must also work together in mission partnership.	Disagree = 1 < > Agree =7 1 2 3 4 5 6 7
13. Submission to Christ as the One Head of the Body inspires you to work together in mission partnership.	Disagree = 1 < > Agree =7 1 2 3 4 5 6 7
14. Scripture teaches that the "Holy Spirit" is the source of all our spiritual gifts.	Disagree = 1 < > Agree =7 1 2 3 4 5 6 7
15. The common calling of all Christians to join God in His mission inspires you to work in mission partnership.	Disagree = 1 < > Agree =7 1 2 3 4 5 6 7
16. Have you offered your giftings/abilities to others in mission partnership?	Never=1 < > Always=7 1 2 3 4 5 6 7
17. Scripture teaches that that the universal Church is made up of all believers in Jesus Christ around the world.	Disagree = 1 < > Agree =7 1 2 3 4 5 6 7
18. The effectiveness of your giftings/abilities is enhanced through mission partnership.	Disagree = 1 < > Agree =7 1 2 3 4 5 6 7
19. Have you pursued organizational working relationships with those outside your organization or church?	Never=1 < > Always=7 1 2 3 4 5 6 7
20. The Bible requires that we work together in mission partnership.	Disagree = 1 < > Agree =7 1 2 3 4 5 6 7

21. Have you chosen to avoid working with other evangelicals because they were not from your own distinctive church or organization?	Never=1 < > Always=7 1 2 3 4 5 6 7
22. Since all gifts come from the Holy Spirit, all gifts are to be used in conjunction with others in mission partnership.	Disagree = 1 < > Agree =7 1 2 3 4 5 6 7
23. Do you live in CAR?	Yes No
24. Is this your first CARC?	Yes No
25. Which continent are you originally from? (Circle one) Asia Africa Europe Australia North America South America	
26. Are you attending as part of an organization or church or coming as an individual? Organization Church Individual	
27. Would you like to clarify or add to any of your answers in this survey? (Please WRITE CLEARLY!) _____ _____ _____	

Thank you for taking the time to respond to this survey! May God bless you as you continue to serve Him.

Many rich blessings,
Kenneth Shreve

Bibliography

Aaker, David A., and George S. Day. *Marketing Research*. 2nd ed. New York: John Wiley & Sons, 1983.

Addicott, Ernie. *Body Matters: A Guide to Partnership in Christian Mission*. Edmonds, WA: Interdev Partnership Associates, 2005.

Alvarez, Carmelo. "Sharing in God's Mission: The Evangelical Pentecostal Union of Venezuela and The Christian Church (Disciples of Christ) in the United States 1960-1980." Dissertation for University of Amsterdam. 10 May 2006. http://dare.ubvu.vu.nl/handle/1871/9807 (1 September 2009).

The Association for Theological Education by Extension and Interdev. *Partnership for Mission: A Degree Level Course*. Bangalore: Taftee/Interdev, 2002.

"Athanasius Creed". http://www.holybible.com/resources/athanasius_creed.htm (4 March 2009).

Baba, Panya. "A Two-Thirds World Perspective: A Case Study." In *Partners in the Gospel: The Strategic Role of Partnership in World Evangelization*, edited by James H. Kraakevik and Dotsey Welliver, 109–116. Wheaton, IL: Billy Graham Center, c. 1992.

Barclay, William. *The Letter to the Romans*. Philadelphia, PA: Westminster Press, 1975.

———. *The Letters to the Galatians and Ephesians*. Philadelphia, PA: Westminster Press, 1975.

———. *The Letters to the Philippians, Colossians, and Thessalonians*. Philadelphia, PA: Westminster Press, 1975.

Barrett, C. K. *Harper's New Testament Commentaries: A Commentary on the First Epistle to the Corinthians*. New York: Harper & Row, 1968.

"Basic Principles: A Synthesis Taken from the United Church of Christ in the Philippines Document 'Partnership in Mission.'" *International Review of Mission* 86, no. 342 (1997): 339–340. http://search.ebscohost.com/login.aspx?direct=true&db=rfh&AN=ATLA0001026483&site=ehost-live (Accessed 21 June 2010).

Baur, Walter. *A Greek-English Lexicon of the New Testament and Other Early Christian Literature*. Translated by William F. Arndt and F. Wilbur Gingrich. Chicago, IL: University of Chicago Press, 1957.

Berding, Kenneth. *What Are Spiritual Gifts: Rethinking the Conventional View*. Grand Rapids, MI: Kregel, 2006.

Boff, Leonardo. *Holy Trinity, Perfect Community*. Maryknoll, NY: Orbis, 2000.

Bosch, David J. *Transforming Mission: Paradigm Shifts in Theology of Mission*. Maryknoll, NY: Orbis Books, 1991.

Brafman, Ori, and Rod A. Beckstrom. *The Starfish and the Spider: The Unstoppable Power of Leaderless Organizations*. New York: Portfolio, 2006.

Breshears, Gerry. "THS 501E Outline: Prolegomena: Topic One – Laying the Foundation for Theology." Class notes: Western Seminary, Portland, OR, May 2006.

Bridge, Donald, and David Phypers. *Spiritual Gifts and the Church*. Downers Grove, IL: InterVarsity, 1973.

Brown, Colin, ed. *The New International Dictionary of New Testament Theology, Vol. 1*. Grand Rapids, MI: Zondervan, 1975.

———. *The New International Dictionary of New Testament Theology, Vol. II*. Grand Rapids, MI: Zondervan, 1971.

———. *The New International Dictionary of New Testament Theology, Vol. III*. Grand Rapids, MI: Zondervan, 1971.

Bruce, F. F. *The Epistle of Paul to the Romans: An Introduction and Commentary*. Grand Rapids, MI: Eerdmans, 1977.

———. *The Epistles to the Colossians, to Philemon, and to the Ephesians*. Grand Rapids, MI: Eerdmans, 1984.

Burdick, Donald W. *The Letters of John the Apostle*. Chicago, IL: Moody Press, 1985.

Bush, Luis. "A Brief Historical Overview of the AD2000 & Beyond Movement and Joshua Project 2000." Paper presented at the North East Asia AD2000/Joshua Project 2000 Consultation in Seoul, 27–30 May 1996. http://www.ad2000.org/histover.htm (Accessed 25 June 2010).

Bush, Luis and Lori Lutz. *Partnering in Ministry: The Direction of World Evangelism*. Downers Grove, IL: InterVarsity, 1990.

Butler, Phill. "Integrated Partnerships." In *Partners in the Gospel: The Strategic Role of Partnership in World Evangelization*, edited by James H. Kraakevik and Dotsey Welliver. Wheaton, IL: Billy Graham Center, c. 1992.

———. *Partnership: Accelerating Evangelism in the 90's*. Ashford, England: Interdev, 1995.

———. "A Survey of Kingdom Collaboration." *Mission Frontiers Magazine*. May-June 2006.

———. *Well Connected*. Waynesboro, GA: Authentic Media, 2005.

Calvin, John. *The Epistle of Paul the Apostle to the Hebrews and the First and Second Epistles of St Peter*. Translated by William B. Johnston. Grand Rapids, MI: Eerdmans, 1963.

Catalyst Services. http://www.catalystservices.org/.

Center for Reformed Theology and Apologetics. "The Nicene Creed." http://www.reformed.org/documents/index.html?mainframe=http://www.reformed.org/documents/nicene.html (Accessed 4 March 2009).

Claydon, Robyn. "Cooperation in Evangelism." *Cooperation in Evangelism II* (1989): 212–215. http://www.lausanne.org/documents/lau2docs/212.pdf (Accessed 2 October 2007).

Cline, Colin Marion. *A Manual of Christian Theology*. Portland, OR: Cutler Printing, 1936.

Clowney, Edmund P. *The Church*. Downers Grove, IL: InterVarsity, 1995.

Consultation on "Partnership in Mission – What Structures?" *International Review of Mission* 81, no. 323 (1992): 467–471. http://search.ebscohost.com/login.aspx?direct=true&db=rfh&AN=ATLA0000861840&site=ehost-live (Accessed 12 June 2010).

"Cooperating in World Evangelization: A Handbook on Church/Para-Church Relationships." *Lausanne Occasional Paper* 24 (March 1983). www.lausanne.org (Accessed 2 October 2007).

Corrie, John, ed. *Dictionary of Mission Theology: Evangelical Foundations*. Downers Grove, IL: InterVarsity, 2007.

Corwin, Gary, and Kenneth B. Mulholland. *Working Together with God to Shape the New Millennium: Opportunities & Limitations*. Pasadena, CA: William Carey Library, 2000.

Creed of Nicea. http://www.thenagain.info/webchron/Mediterranean/ConstanChrist2.html (Accessed 5 March 2009).

Creswell, John W. *Research Design: Qualitative, Quantitative, and Mixed Methods Approaches*. Thousand Oaks, CA: Sage, 2003.

Dana, H. E., and Julius R. Mantey. *A Manual Grammar of the Greek New Testament*. Toronto, Canada: Macmillan, 1927.

Dent, Stephen M. *Partnering Intelligence: Creating Value for Your Business by Building Strong Alliances*. 2nd ed. Palo Alto, CA: Davies-Black, 2004.

Duncan, Graham Alexander. "Partnership in Mission: A Critical Historical Evaluation of the Relationship between 'Older' and 'Younger' Churches." Dissertation for Philosophiae Doctor in the Faculty of Theology, University of Pretoria, April 2007.

Elwell, Walter A., ed. *Evangelical Dictionary of Theology*. Grand Rapids, MI: Baker, 1984.

Erickson, Millard J. *Christian Theology, Vol 1*. Grand Rapids, MI: Baker, 1983.

———. *Christian Theology, Vol 3*. Grand Rapids, MI: Baker, 1985.

———. *Christian Theology*, 2nd ed. Grand Rapids, MI: Baker, 1998.

Fink, Arlene. *The Survey Handbook*. Thousand Oaks, CA: Sage Publications, 1995.

Foulkes, Francis. *Ephesians*. Translated by J. D. Emerson. Grand Rapids, MI: Eerdmans, 1956.

Fowler, Floyd J. *Survey Research Methods*. 3rd ed. Thousand Oaks, CA: Sage, 2002.

Fuller, Lois K. *A Biblical Theology of Missions: God's Great Project for the Blessing of All Nations*. Bukuru, Nigeria: African Christian Textbooks, 2005.

Glass, Gene V., and Julian C. Stanley. *Statistical Methods in Education and Psychology*. Englewood Cliffs, NJ: Prentice-Hall, 1970.
Glasser, Arthur F. *Announcing the Kingdom: The Story of God's Mission in the Bible*. Grand Rapids, MI: Baker, 2003.
Gnanakan, Ken. *Kingdom Concerns: A Theology of Mission Today*. Leicester: IVP, 1993.
Gooding, David. *True to the Faith: A Fresh Approach to the Acts of the Apostles*. London: Hodder & Stoughton, 1990.
Graham, Billy. *Just as I Am*. San Francisco, CA: Harper Collins, 1997.
Grenz, Stanley J. *Revisioning Evangelical Theology: A Fresh Agenda for the 21st Century*. Downers Grove, IL: InterVarsity, 1993.
———. *Theology for the Community of God*. Nashville, TN: Broadman & Holman, 1994.
Grudem, Wayne. *Systematic Theology: An Introduction to Biblical Doctrine*. Leicester: IVP, 1994.
Gundry, Robert H. *A Survey of the New Testament*. Grand Rapids, MI: Zondervan, 1981.
Hackett, David. "Crossing the Will/Skill Divide." *Vision Synergy* (20 May 2009) http://www.visionsynergy.net/864/ (Accessed 5 August 2010).
Hahn, Geoffrey W. "Cross-Cultural Partnerships Characterized by Grace." Unpublished DMin Dissertation, Denver Seminary, April 2007.
Harper, Brad, and Paul Louis Metzger. *Exploring Ecclesiology: An Evangelical and Ecumenical Introduction*. Grand Rapids, MI: Brazos Press, 2009.
Harris, R. Laid, ed., Gleason L. Archer and Bruce K. Waltke, assoc eds. *Theological Wordbook of the Old Testament Vol. 1*. Chicago, IL: Moody Press, 1980.
Harvard Business Review on Strategic Alliances. Boston, MA: Harvard Business Press, 2002.
Henry, Carl F. H. ed. *Basic Christian Doctrines: Contemporary Evangelical Thought*. Grand Rapids, MI: Baker, 1962.
Hiebert, D. Edmond. *The Epistle of James: Tests of a Living Faith*. Chicago, IL: Moody Press, 1979.
———. *First Peter*. Chicago, IL: Moody Press, 1984.
———. *Personalities around Paul*. Chicago, IL: Moody Press, 1973.
Hiebert, Paul. *Anthropological Insights for Missionaries*. Grand Rapids, MI: Baker, 1985.
Hiebert, Paul G., and Frances F. Hiebert. *Case Studies in Missions*. Grand Rapids, MI: Baker, 1987.
Hodge, Charles. *Romans*. Wheaton, IL: Crossway, 1993.
Hughes, Philip Edgcumbe. *The Book of the Revelation: A Commentary*. Leicester: IVP, 1990.
Interdev. *The Power of Partnership*. Interdev, 2002.

Jennings, J. Nelson. "Americans and Missions Today." *Presbyterion* 33, no 2 (2007): 84–93. http://search.ebscohost.com/login.aspx?direct=true&db=rfh&AN=ATLA0001630762&site=ehost-live (Accessed 21 June 2010).
Johnson, Darrell W. *Experiencing the Trinity*. Vancouver, BC: Regent College Publishing, 2002.
Johnson, R. Burke, and Anthony J. Onwuegbuzie. "Mixed Methods Research: A Research Paradigm Whose Time Has Come." *Educational Researcher* 33, no.7 (October 2004): 14–26. http://carbon.videolectures.net/2009/uni_lj/fdv/ssmt09_ljubljana/onwuegbuzie_mmr/MixedMethods.ER.pdf (Accessed 3 October 2009).
Kent, Homer A. *Ephesians: The Glory of the Church*. Chicago, IL: Moody Press, 1971.
Kidner, Derek. *Genesis: An Introduction & Commentary*. Downers Grove, IL: InterVarsity, 1967.
Kistemaker, Simon J. *Exposition of the Epistles of Peter and of the Epistle of Jude*. Hertfordshire, England: Evangelical Press, 1987.
Klein, William W., Craig L. Blomberg, and Robert L. Hubbard. *Introduction to Biblical Interpretation*. Revised and expanded. Nashville, TN: Thomas Nelson, 2004.
Koivisto, Rex A. *One Lord, One Faith: A Theology for Cross-Denominational Renewal*. Eugene, OR: Wipf and Stock, 1993.
Köstenberger, Andreas J., and Scott R. Swain, *Father, Son, Spirit: The Trinity and John's Gospel*. Downers Grove, IL: InterVarsity, 2008.
Kraakevik, James H., and Dotsey Welliver, eds. *Partners in the Gospel: The Strategic Role of Partnership in World Evangelization*. Wheaton, IL: Billy Graham Center, 1992.
The Lausanne Covenant.http://www.lausanne.org/covenant (Accessed 14 April 2010).
The Lausanne Movement. http://www.lausanne.org/global-conversation/whole-gospel-whole-church-whole-world.html (Accessed 14 April 2010).
Lederleitner, Mary T. *Cross-Cultural Partnerships: Navigating the Complexities of Money and Mission*. Downers Grove, IL: InterVarsity, 2010.
Lee, Hong-Jung. "Beyond Partnership, Towards Networking: a Korean Reflection on Partnership in the Web of God's Mission." *International Review of Mission* 91, no. 363 (October 2002): 577–582. http://search.ebscohost.com/login.aspx?direct=true&db=rfh&AN=ATLA0001474077&site=ehost-live (Accessed 21 June 2010).
Letham, Robert. *The Holy Trinity in Scripture, History, Theology, and Worship*. Phillipsburg, NJ: P & R Publishing, 2004.
Lewis, Gordon R., and Bruce A. Demarest. *Integrative Theology*. Grand Rapids, MI: Zondervan, 1996.

Louw, Johannes P., and Eugene A. Nida, eds. *Greek-English Lexicon of the New Testament Based on Semantic Domains*. New York: United Bible Societies 1988, 2nd ed. 1989. Electronic text hypertexted and prepared by OakTree Software, Version 3.7.

Marsh, Colin. "Partnership in Mission: To Send or to Share." *International Review of Mission* 92, no. 366 (2003): 370–381.

Marshall, I. Howard. *Acts*. Grand Rapids, MI: Eerdmans, 1980.

———. *The Epistles of John*. Grand Rapids, MI: Eerdmans, 1978.

Mattessich, Paul W., and Martha Murray-Close. *Collaboration: What Makes It Work*. 2nd ed. Saint Paul, MN: Amherst H. Wilder Foundation, 2001.

Maxwell, John C., and Tim Elmore. *The Power of Partnership in the Church*. Nashville, TN: J. Countryman, Thomas Nelson, 1999.

McGee, J. Vernon. *II Corinthians*. La Verne, CA: El Camino Press, 1977.

McKaughan, Paul. "A North American Response to Patrick Sookhdeo." In *Kingdom Partnerships for Synergy in Missions*, edited by William David Taylor, 67–87. Pasadena, CA: William Carey Library, 1994.

Morris, Leon. *The Gospel according to John*. Grand Rapids, MI: Eerdmans, 1971.

Mounce, Robert H. *The Book of Revelation*. Grand Rapids, MI: Eerdmans, 1977.

Neill, Stephen. *Christian Partnership*. London: SCM Press, 1952.

Newbigin, Lesslie. *The Open Secret: An Introduction to the Theology of Missions*. Grand Rapids, MI: Eerdmans, 1978.

———. *The Open Secret: An Introduction to the Theology of Mission*. rev. ed. Grand Rapids, MI: Eerdmans, 1995.

Nussbaum, Stan. *A Reader's Guide to Transforming Mission*. Maryknoll, NY: Orbis Books, 2005.

O'Brien, Bill. "Cooperation in Evangelism." *Cooperation in Evangelism I* (1989). http://www.lausanne.org/documents/lau2docs/204.pdf (Accessed 2 October 2007).

Orr, William F., and James Arthur Walther. *First Corinthians*. New York: Doubleday, 1976.

Pache, Rene. *The Person and Work of the Holy Spirit*. Chicago, IL: Moody Press, 1954.

Packer, J. I. *Keep in Step with the Spirit*. Old Tappan, NJ: Fleming H. Revell, 1984.

Patterson, Paige. *The Troubled Triumphant Church*. Nashville, TN: Thomas Nelson, 1983.

Patton, Michael Quinn. *Qualitative Research & Evaluation Methods*. 3rd ed. Thousand Oaks, CA: Sage, 2002.

Peters, George W. *A Biblical Theology of Missions*. Chicago, IL: Moody Press, 1972.

Piper, John. *Let the Nations Be Glad: The Supremacy of God in Missions*. Grand Rapids, MI: Baker, 1993.

Power of Connecting. http://www.powerofconnecting.net/.

Pusey, E. B. *The Minor Prophets: A Commentary, Vol 1*. Grand Rapids, MI: Baker, 1950.
Radmacher, Earl D. *What the Church Is All About: A Biblical and Historical Study*. Chicago, IL: Moody Press, 1972.
Rickett, Daniel. *Building Strategic Relationships: A Practical Guide to Partnering with Non-Western Missions*. Pleasant Hill, CA: Klein Graphics Media Center, 2000.
———. *Making Your Partnership Work*. Enumclaw, WA: Wine Press, 2002.
Rowe, Jonathon Y. "Dancing With Elephants: Accountability in Cross-Cultural Christian Partnerships." *Missiology: An International Review* 37, no. 2 (April 2009): 149–163.
Sampley, J. Paul. *Pauline Partnership in Christ*. Philadelphia, PA: Fortress, 1980.
Sauerwein, Daniel. "Inductive Bible Study: A Proposed Program of Study." DMin Dissertation for Western Conservative Baptist Seminary, Portland, OR, 1980.
Shedd, William G. T. *Dogmatic Theology*. 2nd ed. Nashville, TN: Thomas Nelson, 1980.
Simpson, A. B. *Serving the King: Doing Ministry in Partnership with God*. Camp Hill, PA: Christian Publications, 1995.
Shelly, Bruce L. *What Is the Church?* Wheaton, IL: Victor Books, 1978.
Spekman, Robert E., and Lynn A. Isabella, *Alliance Competence: Maximizing the Value of Your Partnerships*. New York: John Wiley & Sons, 2000.
Sproul, R. C. *Knowing Scripture*. Downers Grove, IL: InterVarsity, 1978.
Stott, John R. W. *The Message of Acts*. Leicester: IVP, 1990.
Straus, David. *How to Make Collaboration Work: Powerful Ways to Build Consensus, Solve Problems, and Make Decisions*. San Francisco, CA: Berrett-Koehler Publishers, 2002.
Sunderland, William H., and Issue Group No. 9 on Partnership and Collaboration. "Partnership and Collaboration." *Lausanne Occasional Paper (LOP)* no. 38, Pattaya 2004, copyright 2005, www.lausanne.org (Accessed 2 October 2007).
Taylor, William D., ed. "Partners into the Next Millenium." In *Kingdom Partnerships for Synergy in Missions*. Pasadena, CA: William Carey Library, 1994.
Terry, John Mark, Ebbie Smith, and Justice Anderson. *Missiology*. Nashville, TN: Broadman & Holman, 1998.
Tiessen, Douglas P. "Global Interdependent Ministry Partnerships in the Russian Context." *Mission Studies* 22, no. 1 (2005): 115–134. http://search.ebscohost.com/login.aspx?direct=true&db=rfh&AN=ATLA0001474077&site=ehost-live (Accessed 21 June 2010).
Van Engen, Charles Edward. "Toward a Theology of Mission Partnerships." *Missiology and International Review* 29, no. 1 (2001): 11–44. http://search.ebscohost.com/login.aspx?direct=true&db=rfh&AN=ATLA0001334507&site=ehost-live (Accessed 12 June 2010).

Vine, W. E. *An Expository Dictionary of New Testament Words.* Old Tappan, NJ: Fleming H. Revell, 1966.
Vision Synergy. http://www.visionsynergy.net/.
Wagner, C. Peter. *Lighting the World.* Ventura, CA: Regal Books, 1995.
Wallace, Robert L. *Strategic Partnerships.* Chicago, IL: Dearborn Trade Publishing, 2004.
Wan, Enoch. "The Paradigm of 'Relational Realism.'" *Occasional Bulletin* 19, no. 2 (2006): 1–4.
———. "Relational Theology and Relational Missiology." *Occasional Bulletin of Evangelical Missiological Society* 21, no. 1 (2007): 1–7.
Wan, Enoch, and Mark Hedinger. "Understanding 'Relationality' from a Trinitarian Perspective." *Global Missiology, Trinitarian Studies* (January 2006) www.globalmissiology.org (Accessed 9 April 2008).
Ware, Bruce A. *Father, Son, & Holy Spirit Relationships, Roles, & Relevance.* Wheaton, IL: Crossway, 2005.
Warren, Max. *Partnership: The Study of an Idea.* London: SCM Press, 1956.
Wenger, Etienne, Richard McDermott, and William M. Snyder. *Cultivating Communities of Practice: A Guide to Managing Knowledge.* Boston, MA: Harvard Business Press, 2002.
White, James R. *The Forgotten Trinity.* Minneapolis, MN: Bethany House, 1998.
White, Jerry. *The Church and the Parachurch: An Uneasy Marriage.* Portland, OR: Multnomah, 1983.
Williams, Morris O. *Partnership in Mission: A Study of Theology and Method in Mission.* 1979. Springfield, IL: Division of Foreign Missions, 1986.
Winter, Ralph D. "The Two Structures of God's Redemptive Mission." *Perspectives on the World Christian Movement: A Reader.* 4th ed. Pasadena, CA: William Carey Library, 2009.
Wilson, Fred A. "A New Paradigm for Cross-Cultural Missions." Doctor of Ministry Thesis. Western Conservative Baptist Seminary, June 1994.
Woodbridge, John D., Thomas Edward McComiskey, eds. *Doing Theology in Today's World.* Grand Rapids, MI: Zondervan, 1991.
Wright, Christopher J. H. *The Mission Of God: Unlocking the Bible's Grand Narrative.* Downers Grove, IL: InterVarsity, 2006.
Wright, N. T. *Colossians and Philemon.* Tyndale New Testament Commentaries. Grand Rapids, MI: Eerdmans, 1986.
Wright, Tom. *Paul for Everyone: 2 Corinthians.* Louisville, KY: Westminster John Knox Press, 2004.
Wright, Walter C. *Ephesians.* Chicago, IL: Moody Press, 1954.
Yates, Josh, and Issue Group No 1. "Globalization and the Gospel: Rethinking Mission in the Contemporary World." *Lausanne Occasional Paper* No 30, Pattaya, 2004. Copyright 2005. www.lausanne.org (Accessed 2 October 2007).

Langham Literature and its imprints are a ministry of Langham Partnership.

Langham Partnership is a global fellowship working in pursuit of the vision God entrusted to its founder John Stott –

> *to facilitate the growth of the church in maturity and Christ-likeness through raising the standards of biblical preaching and teaching.*

Our vision is to see churches in the majority world equipped for mission and growing to maturity in Christ through the ministry of pastors and leaders who believe, teach and live by the Word of God.

Our mission is to strengthen the ministry of the Word of God through:
- nurturing national movements for biblical preaching
- fostering the creation and distribution of evangelical literature
- enhancing evangelical theological education

especially in countries where churches are under-resourced.

Our ministry

Langham Preaching partners with national leaders to nurture indigenous biblical preaching movements for pastors and lay preachers all around the world. With the support of a team of trainers from many countries, a multi-level programme of seminars provides practical training, and is followed by a programme for training local facilitators. Local preachers' groups and national and regional networks ensure continuity and ongoing development, seeking to build vigorous movements committed to Bible exposition.

Langham Literature provides majority world preachers, scholars and seminary libraries with evangelical books and electronic resources through publishing and distribution, grants and discounts. The programme also fosters the creation of indigenous evangelical books in many languages, through writer's grants, strengthening local evangelical publishing houses, and investment in major regional literature projects, such as one volume Bible commentaries like *The Africa Bible Commentary* and *The South Asia Bible Commentary*.

Langham Scholars provides financial support for evangelical doctoral students from the majority world so that, when they return home, they may train pastors and other Christian leaders with sound, biblical and theological teaching. This programme equips those who equip others. Langham Scholars also works in partnership with majority world seminaries in strengthening evangelical theological education. A growing number of Langham Scholars study in high quality doctoral programmes in the majority world itself. As well as teaching the next generation of pastors, graduated Langham Scholars exercise significant influence through their writing and leadership.

To learn more about Langham Partnership and the work we do visit **langham.org**

www.ingramcontent.com/pod-product-compliance
Lightning Source LLC
Chambersburg PA
CBHW050758160426
43192CB00010B/1560